islands
of hope

I have set before you life and death,
blessing and curse; therefore choose
life that you and your descendants
may live.

Deuteronomy, 30:19

islands of hope

parks and recreation in environmental crisis

by William E. Brown
for the National Recreation and Park Association

NATIONAL RECREATION AND PARK ASSOCIATION
3101 Park Center Drive, Alexandria, Virginia 22302

The National Recreation and Park Association is a nonprofit organization serving the park and recreation profession and concerned citizens through education and research. It is dedicated to improving the quality of life through effective utilization of human and natural resources. Unless otherwise stated, interpretations and conclusions in NRPA publications are those of the authors. William E. Brown was an environmental consultant in Santa Fe, New Mexico when this manuscript was prepared. Barry S. Tindall, conservation program specialist, NRPA, served as project director. The manuscript was edited by Judith Blakely.

Graphic design by Lester Bounds.

contents

acknowledgements

Main participants and contributors to the two Institutes on Environmental Interpretation included the following persons:

John R. Kinard and James Mayo, Anacostia Neighborhood Museum, Washington, D.C.; Edward P. Alexander and James Short, Colonial Williamsburg, Inc., Williamsburg, Va.; Edward J. Ambry, New Jersey State Council for Environmental Education; Byron L. Ashbaugh, Genesee County, Mich., Parks and Recreation Commission; Charles Westcott, Forest Preserve District, Cook County, Illinois; Preston Schellbach, Macon County, Ill., Conservation District; C. G. Screven, University of Wisconsin; William C. Everhart, Marc Sagan, Steven Lewis, Vernon D. Dame, Gilbert Lusk and Hugh Bell Muller, all with the National Park Service, U.S. Department of the Interior.

These people inspired the ideas and action concepts that form the substance of this book.

Special acknowledgment goes to Raymond L. Nelson, National Park Service, and Barry S. Tindall, National Recreation and Park Association. They conceived and coordinated the Institutes on behalf of their respective organizations. Beyond that, I owe them both very personal debts. Ray's ideas and inspirations got me started on the environmental track, and they are still a large part of anything I can contribute. Barry pulled me through the writing of the book, then served as its editorial conscience.

W. E. B.

preface

This book stems from two Institutes on Environmental Interpretation sponsored by the National Recreation and Park Association. The first Institute met at Chicago in September 1969, the second, in cooperation with the National Park Service, at Harpers Ferry, West Virginia, in May 1970. I participated at Chicago, and, through tapes and manuscript papers, vicariously experienced the Harpers Ferry session.

The basic question that stimulated both Institutes was this: What is the role of the park and recreation profession in this time of environmental crisis?

Answers to this question ranged widely, reflecting different temperaments, backgrounds, and locales. But informing all variations and emphases was this unifying theme: We of this profession must use our talents and resources to help our publics and communities rejoin the natural world.

Basic to this thesis is the assumption that today's social processes contradict, even destroy, the natural processes that sustain man and his companions on this earth. It is understood that nature bats last, that man will not survive unless he limits himself individually and collectively to those actions that conform to nature's unbreakable laws.

The condition of the earth's natural fabric, the state of health of the biosphere, determines man's chances for the good life. A dead world means no human life. A sickly world means degraded human life. A healthy world means at least a chance for quality human life — if humans are smart enough to choose the right options.

Man, through his social organization and technology, has become the principal short-term determinant of the biosphere's state of health. Mainly, man's collective impact has been destructive of the biosphere.

So here we are in a conundrum: The biosphere's state of health determines the range of man's options. At the same time man — the earth's dominant and domineering species — determines the biosphere's state of health.

Given the advanced, accelerating state of environmental crisis, environmental reform can happen only if mankind sets the right priorities soon. But how to set priorities? Which do you start with, the chicken or the egg? Do you save the biosphere first, then reform man? Or do you reform man first, then save the biosphere?

Posing the question forces the answer: Salvation of the biosphere and reform of man must happen simultaneously and symbiotically. We must let the biosphere tell us what to do. Certainly our bossing the biosphere hasn't worked!

To get these instructions and act upon them we must hang on to those remnants of the biosphere that are healthy enough to give instructions. We must learn how to elicit those instructions by becoming students instead of masters. As a species we must adjust our aspirations, our social organizations, and our use of technology to square with the instructions.

This book attempts to focus on these cosmic issues as they relate to the park and recreation resource/profession. Even within this seemingly limited focus the issues are immense. They refuse to stay put in a writer's pigeon-holes. They lap over into other foci, illustrating the inter-relatedness of all things. For this reason the book's organization and sequence, and the rationale for my emphasis on particular topics, must be explained. It all began with some basic questions . . . .

How can the park and recreation profession get into the thick of environmental reform? What are the factors, the means, the resources at its disposal?

The *people* of the profession come first. Their understanding of environmental crisis and their commitment to environmental reform are prerequisites to determined action. The first two chapters speak to these points.

Now the trouble begins. Take the *types of resources* managed by this profession. (Inclusion or exclusion of types bears on definition of the profession itself; e.g., do we include libraries, museums, neighborhood centers, etc.?) Some resources are virtually pristine; others are altered from natural state; still others are completely artificial. Variations multiply as thought probes: small areas, large areas, urban, rural, wilderness, interurban, suburban. There are natural areas, historical areas, recreation areas. These basic categories can be further sub-classified into scores of different types. Jurisdictions begin to intrude: federal park and recreation lands, and the various departments and bureaus that administer them — each moved by differing management priorities and objectives; state and local park and recreation systems — some with scores of areas and thousands of employees, others comprising 10 acres and one custodian.

Thus consideration of just the types of resources managed by the profession balloons into an incredible tangle of types, purposes, and management capabilities and philosophies.

Moving from the resource itself to *the people who use it*, a proliferation of needs and preferences emerges. What will suit a black gang in a ghetto, the jet set, the retiree trailer army, a school group?

Finally, what are the different potentials for environmental management and communications at the different types of resources, which serve so many different types of clientele?

To get order out of this chaos of variables I have arbitrarily simplified in this fashion: *First*, the type of *experience* that visitors get in a park or recreation area is the critical thing — not the administrative classification, size, or jurisdiction. From this premise I developed a broad classification scheme for park and recreation areas based on the *dimensions of life* that visitors can

7

experience in such areas. *Second,* I centered on three *means of environmental action and communication* that this profession can use to make its resources centers for environmental reform. *Third,* through *case studies and scenarios,* I attempted to combine these factors (dimensions and means) so that they apply directly or by inference to a broad spectrum of park and recreation managers, properties, and clientele.

Now let us examine this schema and the way it affected the organization of this book.

The mainstream of the park and recreation resource/profession comprises four dimensions: natural, historical, recreation, and social. These dimensions are not mutually exclusive; rather they define the *basic purposes* for which properties have been set aside for public use, whatever the blending of dimensions in actual operations at a given property.

If people are to rejoin the natural world, they need experience in these four dimensions of life:

The *natural dimension* gives perspective —

> on nature's workings, the mystery of the web of life;
> on man as one species among many, all living interdependently off the bounty of the earth;
> on the individual as an integral part of this total system — both biologically and spiritually.

The *historical dimension* gives perspective —

> on cultures of the past, particularly as expressions of alternate value systems;
> on the relationships of cultures, to each other and to the rest of nature;
> on the cultural options chosen that produced success or failure.

The *recreation dimension* gives perspective —

> on the amenities of life off the treadmill, including both strenuous and serene involvement in natural settings;
> on individual physical and mental health;
> on the joy of play, whether experienced as water recreation at a remote reservoir or a game of sandlot ball in a city park.

The *social dimension* gives perspective —

> on group relationships of play and community activities;
> on social reconstruction, particularly in city neighborhoods;
> on the unexpected fun of meeting compatible strangers in the park and recreation context, as opposed to formal social associations.

The different types of park and recreation resources managed by this profession offer experiences in four dimensions. The challenge is to make these experiences relevant to environmental crisis and catalysts for environmental reform on a broad front that blends natural and social processes into one system — the total environment.

That brings us to the means of environmental action and communication. These means are *environmental management, environmental interpretation,* and *environmental education.*

Environmental management is an extremely broad concept, and it is the base for environmental interpretation/education. It concerns not only specific management practices inside a park or recreation area; it reaches beyond the boundaries to involve the public in *action* to conserve the area and its regional context. As such, environmental management is the fundamental means of environmental action and communication.

A basic task of environmental management is to "hang on to those remnants of the biosphere that are healthy enough to give instructions." Therefore, the emphasis in Chapter III is on the in- and out-boundary work of conserving prime natural areas and their regional contexts. This emphasis does not imply disregard of environmental management principles in other types of areas. Areas that are basically altered from natural state (a reservoir, an historic site) and those that are completely artificial (a mid-city park, a rehabilitated dump) deserve the same care for ecology and esthetics as a pristine natural area. But the starting points and the management emphases in non-pristine areas are basically different, reflecting man-caused alterations of environment and different dimensions of experience to be had there.

Chapters IV and V, Environmental Interpretation and Environmental Education, deal principally with the formal means of environmental communication. Such means exploit the dimensions of life experienced in the park or recreation area to help visitors and school children develop an environmental ethic. These formal communications are meant to lead to action; they are not simply intellectual exercises. Thus, the adult visitor or school child who possesses an environmental ethic uses it as a standard to judge and influence environmental action back home.

More directly action-oriented is the brand of environmental interpretation/education that occurs in the social dimension. Applicable mainly in urban poverty areas, the theme here is environmental reform through community action and social reconstruction in the neighborhood of the park or recreation area.

In the pages that follow I shall explore controversial topics, for no profound discussion of environmental reform can avoid controversy; nor can park and recreation people stimulate reform from the safety of the sidelines. Chapter VI, therefore, concentrates on the new personal and organizational flexibilities that this profession must cultivate if it is to maintain cohesion in a context of internal and external stress. The book concludes with a Readings and Resources Appendix for missionary recruits.

Many are the limitations of this book, beginning with its author, who started as a National Park Service historian, then became an environmental specialist in the Service's Southwest Regional Office, then became a free-lance environmental writer and activist. Fortunately, my work in park and interpretive planning, management appraisal, and environmental affairs crossed many lines and forced me to work with many disciplines, in and out of the Service.

Further limitations include the factor of time. The National Recreation and Park Association believes that the results of the two Institutes on Environmental Interpretation should spread through the profession quickly, because neither we nor our environment can wait around. This objective obviates time for comprehensive research and pre-publication critique among the profession. It dictates a narrative distillation of Institute proceedings, rather than a ponderous editing and cross-checking of the proceedings. And it means that this work is less a true synthesis than one man's view of the synthesis, which is risky because my mind selects things in its own perverse way.

For myself, I view this task, which should be frightening, with a degree of equanimity. For I see this book as an essay, as a provocation, as an opener in what hopefully will become an ever more vigorous dialogue within the park and recreation profession. If this happens, weaknesses and errors will be found out; strengths and truths will be built upon.

Finally, I wish to thank the National Recreation and Park Association for giving me this opportunity to express myself as well as to compile the expressions of others. To the extent possible I have attributed major ideas and statements to the authors. But given the wide range of sources consulted, many who contributed indirectly could not be named. Thanks to you all!

William E. Brown
Santa Fe, New Mexico
December 1970

interlude I

thoughts on the unthinkable

"Business as usual is suicide."

Barry Commoner

The heart of the present dilemma is this: Despite massive educational campaigns by scientists, philosophers, and the public media, we refuse to face squarely the real meaning of environmental crisis. As a species we learned long ago to close our minds against the unthinkable. Sanity demanded it. Now we must stretch our consciousness and our strength to confront the unthinkable. For it is a paradox that in the qualitatively new world we have wrought, sanity and survival demand it.

The biosphere shakes like a strained muscle from the stresses put upon it by man. Man-made systems, their foundations trembling in the sands of environmental ignorance, ever more frequently fail. Individual people crack under the aggregating strains. Communities, neighborhoods falter and die. Nations bare their teeth and seek security in destruction.

With these warning signals raging about us, we continue to hug old patterns of behavior and action. Somehow we'll muddle through. Business as usual.

The facts say otherwise. They say that man will disappear from this earth— dragging with him the rest of the living host—unless he radically changes his value systems, and the behaviors and actions that stem from them.

The park and recreation profession, like other groups, is caught in the current of business as usual. There are but two choices: Either we slide complacently into the maelstrom, or we inspire ourselves and others to strike for the shore.

chapter I

environmental crisis and the new professional mission

The rhetoric and the facts of environmental crisis are with us like a plague. Technical journals, magazines, books, TV specials, political speeches batter us with prophesies of doom. Business and industry respond with soothing advertisements. Governments pass laws.

Youth declares them all frauds. They point to the Santa Barbara oil slick, the depredations of mining, timbering, agribusiness, and the power industry. They label "conservation" agencies brokers for the special interests that consume the common wealth of land, air, and water.

A whole new environmental law profession makes the scene. Teachers and Chambers of Commerce organize clean-up days. Students petition city councils to stop the polluters. Radicals and blacks curse the environmental fad because it diverts money and energy from peace and poverty programs.

Cities crumble into chaos, and the sense of community dies in riots, racism, and hot words of hate.

Engineers and scientists search their souls, assessing their responsibility for the technology and inventions they have given to governments.

Conservation groups themselves lack agreement on the priorities of environmental salvation. They fight one symptom while the system mass produces a hundred new ones.

Anti-environmentalists strike back: The business of America is business, whatever the Jeremiahs say.

Business magazines editorialize that pollution control is the growth industry of the future, all the while projecting greater demands for power, production, consumption—thus assuring the need for pollution control.

Battles rage over pollution-control tax advantages, over industry vs. consumer payment of the environmental debit.

Politicians hop on the bandwagon and search their opponents' voting records to prove their own environmental virtue.

Governors proclaim their concern for environmental quality, then lure industry with loose pollution-control laws.

Bureaucrats say they lack authority to clean up.

It's the Black Hats vs. the White Hats. It's a cacaphony of shouting and finger-pointing and viewing with alarm. It's a stew of contradictions and cross-purposes.

There is reason for this racket. For the environmental crisis cuts to the bone of the operational values and successes of our society. On every side we see the conflict between what worked yesterday and what must be done today if there is to be a tomorrow. We are at decision point. But with few exceptions we have neither individually nor collectively decided to substantially modify our beliefs and life ways to meet the environmental imperative.

What is that imperative? It is simply this: The biosphere is finite and fragile. Men look upon it as though it were infinite and elastic. Further, they look upon themselves as special creations independent of the web of life. So they damage and cut the strands of this web, which is their only support in the surrounding abyss of dead space.

As the physical environment goes down the number of people goes up. Competition between the haves and have nots gets rougher—locally and on the world stage. Human life tends to get nasty, brutish, and short. For human life, as a part of nature, can't help reflecting the general degradation of nature. Mankind's chances for the good life diminish as the natural base of life diminishes.

Up to this point many people can agree. Most of us can join in the handwringing phase. But beyond this point the going gets rough. For now the question must be asked: Where do we draw the line; what do we do without?

The complex of forces and powers that drives us to produce more and more electricity illustrates the whole problem. Electricity structures the very foundations of our society. All industrial processes, even those that produce other forms of energy, depend on electricity. Predictions of the future show the demand for electricity doubling, trebling, quadrupling over the next 30 years. Built into these predictions are the production of more steel and aluminum, more automobiles, bigger cities, more fertilizer, more agriculture—more people. Industry needs electricity to make more things for more consumers, who run their new things with electricity. Governments join with utilities to build new power plants to meet the predicted demands. Power plants themselves must be powered. This means more dams, more strip mines, more nuclear reactors. Water and land resources bend under the pressure of more extraction. Air, already loaded, takes on more thousands of tons of particulates and poisonous chemicals, along with radioactive wastes.

The Scientists' Institute for Public Information, in *Environmental Cost of Electric Power*[1], bluntly asserts

---

[1] Scientists' Institute for Public Information, New York, 1970

that our environment can't take this unrestrained growth of electric power. Each of the principal means of power generation (hydroelectric, fossil-fuel, nuclear fission) burdens the natural fabric so brutally that the assumption of growth itself must be challenged. And it will be decades before finer, less demanding power technology (solar, nuclear fusion, geo-thermal) can begin to meet even present levels of consumption.

So we have to go back to that nasty question: What do we do without? It must be understood—despite the assumptions, predictions, and interlocking forces that press us remorselessly toward more power production—that *this is not a question about alternative means for getting more power.* The question means what it says: What do we do without? What current uses of electric power are wasteful and should be stopped? What uses are really necessary and efficient? Because we must begin to live within a power budget, and this budget must be set on the basis of bio-economics. How much power can we produce without destroying the natural fabric (including ourselves), or preferably, without so damaging the biosphere that quality life is impossible?

If these basic questions are not faced, if they are not answered and actions taken upon the answers, then environmental management, interpretation, and education are meaningless. It does no good to take refuge in the old-style conservation fight that averts a power plant in one place, only to have five more go up someplace else. For depredations upon the environment anywhere affect us all. And it is only a matter of time before the overlapping ill effects from such depredations homogenize the debased quality of the common air, water, and land—with consequent ill effects upon individual and social health.

This is heady stuff. Before the world got so small it used to be enough for park and recreation people to protect the properties under their management: Don't build that road (pipe line, factory . . .) in my park! What goes on outside my boundary I can't help. Period.

But now the rules have changed. Because the simplest understanding of ecology makes us aware that no park or recreation resource can exist unimpaired if its natural context is degraded or destroyed and its social context is human misery and discontent. Nor do boundaries themselves have any real meaning today. Air and water circulate through, under, and above boundaries. What happens to the land upstream affects all land downstream. Add the fate of mammals, birds, fish. Add, too, people.

If most people live in cities like today's cities, they are divorced (it seems) from the natural processes upon which they depend. Insulating social processes and tools (the supermarket, the air-conditioner) seem to be the real world. The fact that all of these social processes and products reach back for their beginnings to the earth, the air, and the water is forgotten. Also forgotten is the fact that the sun is the ultimate source of all the animate and inanimate energy that people expend. And the sun grows dimmer these days.

This thing about people goes to the guts of it. People adapt themselves to ugliness and stress. So what good are esthetically pleasing places, serene places? People in cities think power comes from a power plant, not from a river, or a coal mine, or a chunk of uranium. If the power fails they blame the guy who runs the power plant, instead of looking deeper to the struggling earth itself. People who survive the urban rat-race by swinging elbows and crowding out their neighbors bring these same survival tactics to park and recreation areas. Thus does law enforcement become the preoccupation of park management. On and on it goes. But it boils down to this: Park and recreation resources must appeal to increasingly urbanized, socially insulated people (whether living in urban, suburban, or rural places) in ways that convince these people that they must continue to have and support such resources. Without them the esthetics and perspectives of the natural world will be lost, the chance to understand and compare other cultures and historical eras will be lost, the amenities of life off the treadmill will be lost.

Most important, if there are no more exceptional places where the esthete, the scientist, and the person seeking joy can go, the future surely will be diminished. There simply have to be places where people can experience alternatives to the current headlong rush to oblivion. Think about it: If the *experience* of alternatives is lost, the very *idea* that there are alternatives may go too.

What can we do about it? How can we use our resources to help save the world, the task which is prerequisite to perpetuation of our resources?

This brings us to the matter of a new, at least greatly expanded, professional mission. If the ideas so far discussed have validity, then the notion of the park and recreation *mission* is self-evident. The properties we manage include the quality environments still left to mankind. They are the places where, if it can happen at all, the social and natural processes can be brought together in a new synthesis that conduces to the survival, the quality, and the simple joy of life. Unless we do our best to bring about this synthesis we will have failed morally, because we didn't plow back into society the dividends of one of its wisest investments. And we will have failed pragmatically, because a world reduced to bare survival (destruction waiting in the wings) will have no room for parks and recreation.

It is this blending of motive—moral and pragmatic—that tempers our mission. And it is the notion of mission that urges us to speak and act forthrightly on the great issues of our time. Finally, it cannot be escaped that the sum of these issues is the restructuring of society to the end that men make peace among themselves and with the earth.

interlude II

beginning
where we can

. . . and while many people are
getting involved in the fight to
save the environment, John Kennedy
of Edinburgh, Scotland, has invented
a pair of electric shoes to solve
his problem of chronic cold feet.

News Item
Environment, May 1970

Mr. Kennedy's cold feet speak to us all. So does his positive action.

We are conditioned to accept the societal frame and work within it, rather than being catalyst—along with others— for rebuilding the frame. Yet the most cursory reading of environmental literature shows the need for establishing new assumptions about man's place in the web of life, then taking action that squares with these new assumptions. We cannot escape, except by default, the call to throw our talents and resources into the fray. Because . . .

This profession is founded on the ideal of ennobling human life. The places we manage are those places where the whole man—physical, thoughtful, joyful—can reach toward fulfillment. We have a tradition of getting him started toward fulfillment through educational and interpretive programs.

Now our duties extend beyond the visitor, as such, to mankind at large. Now our parks become models of environmental quality, samplers where quality life in both the ecological and social senses can be experienced. They are the existing contrasts to prevailing ecological unwisdom—unwisdom that is destroying not only the "natural world," but also that part of it most important to us, humanity itself.

As exemplars of quality environment and life, our areas provide the larger society a standard to strive for—not just in special places, but also in the ordinary places where people live their daily lives.

The educational responsibility implied in this vision—park and recreation resources as catalysts for *general* environmental reform—is enough to give us all cold feet. But consistent with previous discussion, electric shoes are out.

chapter II

environmental reform –commitment and goals

In the main, this book aims at a profession employed by governments—local, state, federal. Public employees tend to wear pretty snug wraps when controversy comes along. The notion of positive engagement in the environmental reform movement, which is very controversial, causes an instinctive fumbling for the OFF switch.

Particularly is this so given the broad interpretation of environment used throughout this work: population, poverty, racial discrimination, politics, the automobile, national priorities, war, military-industrial complex, pesticides, detergents, air and water quality, taxes, industry and business, economic growth, standard of living (how gross is the gross national product?), quality of life, legal and administrative regulation, institutional inertia, and so on. These terms and phrases—individually, selectively, collectively—intrude in any serious discussion of environment. Each one of them is worth a punch in the nose from someone. And after the initial pain come thoughts of career, kids in college, and the like.

Each person in the profession has to decide the level of his own commitment (read controversy) in the environmental reform struggle. All of us have faced, will face more, the inner torment of rationalization, trying to do what we think is right and courageous. We have argued, will argue more, the pros and cons of standing firm where it really counts, yet preserving effectiveness for future engagements. After all, if you get fired or dead-ended what influence do you have?

The pressures within any bureaucracy—from top to bottom—tend strongly to favor those who *don't* rock the boat. Yet the times call for armies of Don Quixotes, for self-radicalized organizations that can quickly respond to radical new demands.

Individually and organizationally, we as a profession have a lot of the "business as usual" syndrome to overcome— *if* our promise as contributors to environmental reform is to be realized.

So how do we inspire ourselves to get moving?

This same question besets everyone who is concerned—not just us. Scientists, lawyers, doctors wrestle with it. Universities, businesses, and industries wrestle with it. And from this inner torment, which surfaces increasingly in public statements and acts, is developing a broadened societal consensus for honest confrontation with environmental realities.

Because the state of the environment will worsen before it gets better (collectively, *Homo sapiens* hasn't begun to reverse the destructive trends of his own makings), we can expect the societal consensus to expand rapidly in the near future. This is true because environmental insults are beginning to really hurt large segments of the population previously insulated from them. The reality of the global village, where no one can escape pollution and the wrath of human misery, descends upon even those whose money and mobility kept them clean and safe before. Witness the smog, commuter problems, and surge of crime that beset suburbia. Witness the poisons from agriculture, food processing, medicines, and ubiquitous radiation that make no distinctions between rich and poor. Witness the deterioration of yesterday's refuges from ugliness—parks, resorts, and the charter-flight outbacks of the world.

There simply is no place left where one can get away from it all. The fact that we are all in one lifeboat becomes more evident every day. Pretty soon, the passengers who keep chopping holes in it, and the ones who don't help stop them, will be the minority.

In another one of those paradoxes that afflict situations of stress, it might be said that people who risk rocking the boat now, to prevent others from chopping holes in it, will end up with the survivors.

This is not a flippant essay on risk. It is deadly serious. Without inner conviction that deep and even dangerous commitment to environmental reform has immediate relevance to survival, prestige, and career, few people will take the leap. When it becomes plain that inaction means culpability both within the individual conscience *and* in the full light of society's critical gaze, then the urge to participate becomes socially acceptable and compelling—not some clandestine, subversive radicalism to be avoided by the good bureaucrat.

In sum, when times get tough, and they will get tougher, there are those who jump in to help, and those who don't.

The park and recreation profession is better informed on environmental matters than the general public—this is our business; it is idealistically motivated to preserve, to fight for the betterment of, the environment and the quality of human life; it manages for the people critically important environmental oases; and it has the image of stalwart honesty and courage symbolized by the ranger who loves and protects his land. It would be a pity if such a chosen group failed to join the vanguard.

Hortatory preachments get awfully tiresome—especially when directed at people who consider themselves already in the vanguard. It hurts to think that people who have devoted their careers to conservation and healthy recreation should be subject to criticism, prodded to do more. Yet that is the basic purpose of this book, which is faithful to the spirit of the Institutes that inspired it, because the state of the world has changed qualitatively since most of our careers began.

A few years ago, particularly in the United States, it seemed that society could manage its affairs. Now there is doubt. A few years ago it was enough to follow society's dictates and mind our own business. But now society is suffering from major illness; and this profession, managing the healthy environments that can be society's medicine, is on the spot. It must do more as diagnostician of society's ills and as dispenser of health, through exemplary environmental management, interpretation, and education.

We have to help lead society toward environmental wisdom—even if sometimes it means being contrary and cantankerous. To date, with few exceptions, the profession has failed in this leadership role. A few strong voices, yes. But too few and too timid for the work at hand.

To show how short we fall as a profession from the leadership role demanded, let's sample a few pronouncements from other professions and institutions of our society—including some that would seem to have the greatest stake in the status quo!

> Basic to all solutions is the need for a new way of thinking. So far, the key to so-called progress has been man's ability to focus his energies on a single problem, whether fighting a war or going to the moon. But thinking in compartments is the road to environmental disaster. Americans must view the world in terms of unities rather than units. To recognize the interdependence of all creatures is to

see all kinds of follies—from the one-occupant cars that choke highways to the tax policies that discourage mass transit and land preservation.

The biggest need may be a change in values; the whole environmental problem stems from a dedication to infinite growth on a finite planet. . . .

Time, February 2, 1970, p. 63*

. . . Luce . . . is a new breed in the boardroom—an executive who can actually contemplate the notion that America might have to ease up its insatiable pursuit of material goods in order to have another kind of good life. It may be necessary, he said last week, to do without some "frills"—including frills that use electricity—to avoid those "aspects of the good life that are threatening to engulf us."

Newsweek, July 13, 1970, p. 81**
quoting Charles F. Luce,
Chairman of the Board,
Consolidated Edison Co.

We must begin to do something, for it is already clear that the effects of air and water pollution may be serious and even fatal. A "shoot now, we'll see what we hit later" outlook is indefensible. To await complete verification of the relationship between pollution and disease is certainly not justified. The evidence is sufficiently incriminating to state that a relationship does exist, and that pollution is a significant contributory cause of the major diseases now preventing the increased longevity of Americans. Prudence dictates that measures must be taken at this time to decrease these hazards to urban man.

Saturday Review, July 4, 1970, p. 49
quoting Dr. Bertram W. Carnow, M.D.,
University of Illinois College of Medicine

It is particularly fitting that my first official act in this new decade is to approve the National Environmental Policy Act.

Richard M. Nixon,
January 1, 1970

. . . all agencies of the Federal Government shall—

(A) utilize a systematic, interdisciplinary approach which will insure the integrated use of the natural and social sciences and the environmental design arts in planning and in decisionmaking which may have an impact on man's environment; . . .

(F) make available to States, counties, municipalities, institutions, and individuals, advice and information useful in restoring, maintaining, and enhancing the quality of the environment; . . .

from Title I, *National Environmental Policy Act of 1969*

Predictably, the public outcry against environmental pollution has goaded big industrial polluters into striking back with expensive image-cleansing advertising campaigns.

In today's climate of distrust of large institutions, the polluters are asking for trouble.

Standard Oil Company is already under investigation by the state for claiming that a new gasoline formula, with F-310 additive, is a "significant step" toward solving the smog problem. . . .

Fortney H. Stark, Jr.
President, Security National Bank,
Oakland, California, in
The Sense of Security
bank newsletter, April-May, 1970

The chairman of the board of the Bank of America [Louis B. Lundborg] cited the lessons to be drawn from the turmoil in which his mighty establishment has been embroiled with the students of the University of California at Santa Barbara. He bluntly rejected the conspiratorial nonsense peddled by the Nixon Administration. "We are facing a real, honest-to-God disenchantment," he warned. "Not just a passing, momentary flare-up that will go away if we keep it cool for a while."

The beginning of wisdom, and perhaps the beginning of peace, Lundborg said, requires the Rotarians to recognize:

"That the violence must be rejected but the dissent and the protest must not be.

"That there is a new value system emerging in America starting with the youth but becoming one of the new facts of life for the rest of us to deal with.

"Our dealing with it will jar us out of most of the comfortable assumptions that we have grown up with all our lives."

If it is ironic that this perception should be stated by a banker addressing Rotarians when it seems to have been lost among those who are presumed to be the custodians of our culture, it is nevertheless encouraging.

Some of the most outraged and perceptive cries are now being heard in unlikely places. . . .

> from the Harry S. Ashmore *
> syndicated column, July 5, 1970

CRONKITE: The hoopla of Earth Day is over. The problems remain. Only time will tell if these demonstrations accomplished anything. Now, let's summarize the points that were brought home today to a lot of people who have missed the point so far.

For instance, the militants, who see all this as an establishment trick to divert attention from what to them are more urgent concerns, like civil rights and like Vietnam, they seemed to have missed the point that there are no civil rights or peace in a lifeless world.

For instance, the politicians who see this as a "safe" crusade, they seem to have missed the point that it will involve treading on more special interests than ever in our history. For the first time, they may even have to come out against motherhood.

For instance, those in industry who see the crisis as only the hysterical creation of do-gooders, they've missed the point if they haven't heard the unanimous voice of the scientists warning that halfway measures and business-as-usual cannot possibly pull us back from the edge of the precipice.

For instance, the too-silent majority. The greatest disappointment today was the degree of nonparticipation across the country, and especially the absence of adults. And the young people who did participate were in a skylark mood, which contrasted rudely with the messages of apocalypse.

Those who ignored Earth Day, well, that's one thing. Those who ignore the crisis of our planet, that's quite another. The indifferent have missed the point, that to clean up the air and earth and water in the few years science says is left to us means personal involvement and may mean personal sacrifice the likes of which Americans have never been asked to make in time of peace.

The sense of today's teach-in was that America must undertake a revolution in its way of life. Affluent America will, we were told, almost certainly have to scale down its standards of living, give up having as

many cars, as many children, as many cans, as many
conveniences, as much conspicuous consumption. . . .

That's what today's message really means. And those
who marched today and those who slept and those
who scorned are in this thing together. What is at
stake and what is in question is survival.

> Walter Cronkite, CBS News Special,
> *Earth Day: A Question of Survival*

So endeth the reading. But doesn't it get to you
that some of today's bank presidents and bureaucrats
call a spade a spade? That doctors and commentators,
vulnerable to public and professional reprisal, say tough,
unpleasant things? That Congress and the President buy
the gospel, if not yet the price tag of environmental
reform?

Not quoted here were many we have read before—
scientists, some of them working on government-
sponsored projects, who question the government's
wisdom, even its veracity regarding those projects;
lawyers, like Ralph Nader and Victor Yannacone, Jr.,
who challenge their profession to get into the fight, then
go out and show how it's done.

Each day evidence mounts that an expanding
societal consensus for environmental reform is with us.
People who talk straight don't always get ostracized;
many get respect and get things done. Sitting tight is
unrewarding these days. In other words the switch to
honest—sometimes blunt and unpleasant—environmental
activism is on. It's the time to separate men from boys,
wheat from chaff, fishing from cutting bait. *Now* is that
time.

Granted that freedom and risk go together (even in
an atmosphere of expanding freedom), that freedom
must be our choice, that risk for great goals is worth it,
that being aligned with the risk-takers is to choose life
and oppose death—what next?

The tactics of environmental reform for the park and recreation profession come under the headings Environmental Management, Environmental Interpretation, and Environmental Education. These are the headings for the next three chapters, which form the body of this book. Before diving into these topics (which are inextricably interwoven), let us summarize the goals of our profession in the environmental reform movement:

First, on a greatly expanded base of public support—which we initiate—we defend fearlessly all assaults from without on the integrity of the areas we manage. We hold in trust the last remnants of society's quality-environment bank account—the gene pool, if you will, of the healthy world of tomorrow.

Second, we reform internal management policies and techniques to avert our own mistakes and weaknesses. Inadvertence, ignorance, malfeasance in the name of park management can be as destructive as the assault from without.

Third, having secured a quality-environment base—protected from predation, overuse, and ourselves—we help the larger society to use that base (a) to develop an environmental ethic and (b) to establish quality-environment standards for application throughout society. This is the catalytic function that helps man reconstruct the web of life *where he lives and works day by day*.

Fourth, we recognize that healthy natural processes cannot be reestablished and sustained by a society that is divided, disorganized, and despairing. Therefore, we use our park and recreation areas as a base for greatly expanded community action to alleviate human misery and deprivation. Such efforts may center on the urban park and recreation scene, but they must also transcend that scene. It would be unworthy of this profession—and of national, state, and local jurisdictions—if poor people continue to be effectively excluded from nonurban park and recreation experiences.

These goals finally blend into one supreme goal: the affirmation of life through the naturalization of social processes. This naturalization is a compound of intertwined negative and positive factors. Negatively, man trims his actions to fit nature's limits. Positively, he works with nature and himself (society) to reestablish environmental diversity and health, thus enriching human life.

interlude III

the seamless whole

The human environment is an immense complex of natural elements, man-made structures, institutions, societies and other people. . . . Environmental quality and human welfare are not two independent evaluations. They are two views of the same system of interactions. It is not possible for one to remain good while the other is bad.

Dr. Frederick E. Smith
Harvard University
"Scientific Problems and Progress in
  Solving the Environmental Crisis"
February 19, 1970

This profession bases its environmental conservation/reform mission on the holistic nature of the web of life. Understood is the fact that no single strand can be broken without weakening the whole structure. All of our efforts begin with, are based upon, the unifying concept of environmental management. Two interdependent thrusts turn that concept into results: First, we preserve and manage park and recreation lands in a way that creates a quality-environment base. Second, from that base we convey environmental knowledge and standards to the public.

The philosophy that guides our environmental management is the philosophy that the whole family of man must eventually adopt. This philosophy is rooted in the ethic proclaimed by Aldo Leopold—an ethic that "changes the role of *Homo sapiens* from conqueror of the land-community to plain member and citizen of it."

Through environmental management our stewardship of society's environmental gene pools produces a paramount result: upgraded park and recreation lands, administered and operated by environmentally sensitive people. In turn these quality environments become exemplars to be emulated by managers of other environments.

This philosophy reaches park and recreation personnel through the media of policy statements, planning documents, and training programs. We express this philosophy in the way we do our daily work of planning, development, administration, maintenance, protection, and interpretation. Concession personnel are similarly aided to implement environmental management in their daily work.

For the public, this philosophy is articulated by interpretive and educational programs. Such programs include the traditional media and messages of formal on- and off-site presentations. But more importantly, they include a new substantive involvement of the public in environmental conservation/reform *action* designed to protect park and recreation areas.

Visitors to park and recreation areas experience the ultimate meaning of environmental management in the quality environments they find and the dimensions of life they experience in these areas.

This management philosophy derives from a total-environment approach that recognizes the interrelationships and interdependencies that bind park and recreation people and lands to the larger physical and social environment.

Environmental management makes us and the resources we manage relevant to the evolving society of which we are a part. Only thus can the park and recreation complex survive. For irrelevance means discard. And if management of the total environment fails, no part of the total environment can survive unimpaired.

chapter III

environmental management

The essence of environmental management is the holistic view that ties resources, people, and surroundings into a functioning, healthy ecosystem. In 1968 the U.S. House of Representatives Subcommittee on Science, Research, and Development published a report, *Managing the Environment*,[1] which summarized the reasons for environmental *mis*-management. One statement in particular rings loud and clear:

> It is difficult to evaluate changes or uses for immediate gain in terms of their eventual effect on the status of the environment. There are conflicts when environmental quality is managed by different policies originating in conservation, agriculture, esthetics, recreation, economic development, human health, and so forth. An overall policy for the environment must be established which integrates these purposes and objectives and which provides for choice when they are incompatible.

This need for overall, integrated policy is reflected on the national level by the National Environmental Policy Act of 1969, by the creation of a supradepartmental Environmental Protection Agency, and by

[1]Report to the Committee on Science and Astronautics, U.S. House of Representatives, Washington, 1968.

a host of other efforts designed to avert the spastic left-hand/right-hand contradictions built into government operations.

But we need not go to the top for examples of mis-management based on non-integrated planning, development, and operations. With few exceptions, men act today (in the individual park or in any other entity) in a non-net, single-line manner—philosophically, culturally, technologically. They take the shortest route from A to B, even though it disrupts the net of interrelationships between the two points.

Thus, even today, the typical park or recreation area is managed on the premise that administration, maintenance, protection, and interpretation are separate functions, rather than facets of an integrated whole. Thus does a planner or designer, unaware of ecologic factors at the site, encourage developments that are the curse of park managers and maintenancemen. Thus do builders destroy scenery and habitats in the very act of constructing access to them. Thus do wildlife managers, sponsored by hunters, violate ecosystems to increase the game harvest. Thus do programmers and budget directors set priorities and allocations that force park managers into shoddy, environmentally destructive operations.

These linear modes of action lead to disregard of by-product consequences to the total net of man/man and man/environment relationships. Thus do *by-products* become the true, the significant products of otherwise-directed action.

Chance rules in this linear context.

Environmental management aims to *discover* the factors of man/man and man/environment relationships within a specific entity or region; to *understand* how these factors relate as parts of a network; to *act* in light of these relationships—so that significant results of a proposed action are known *before* the act takes place.

Only in this way can people actually get the future they set out to get. *The main object of environmental management is to replace chance with rational process and predictable result.*

The first step on the road to environmental management is to change man/man relationships (the substance and forms of human and organizational interaction). Today we are handicapped in getting holistic solutions to man/environment problems because our educational, professional, and vocational systems produce categorized men who work in pigeon-holes and produce categorized, out-of-context solutions.

The human ecology of environmental management aims to break down existing categories by pulling together people who, in inter-disciplinary fashion, cross-fertilize and cross-check each other to produce in-context solutions. Not only does this mode of operation produce better solutions; it requites the venturesome minds now frustrated in organizational pigeon-holes.

¶ Discussion of the nuts and bolts of environmental management is so much pie in the sky unless current management systems and practices are radically changed. Today's human, organizational, institutional, and political arrangements seem purposely designed to frustrate environmental management. What, then, are the obstacles within ourselves, within our respective organizations and jurisdictions—and beyond them—that prevent creation of a receptive context for environmental management?

At the center is this problem: Whether at the national, state, or local level, park and recreation resources rank low on society's priority list—as measured by allocation of tax dollars. This low priority reflects a political judgment that park and recreation resources are a desirable but peripheral social investment. This judgment in turn stems largely from our own professional perpetuation of a limited, obsolete role in the crises of our times. Only rarely, for example, do park and recreation people and resources reach into the seething ghettos with lasting impact—meaning more than putting up another basketball hoop. Nor have we tapped in significant ways the frustrated idealism of youth, whether zealous students or our own young recruits. Nor have we begun to exploit the real value of our resources to the scientific, educational, and political communities as testing grounds for applied environmental reform (as opposed to traditional academic field trips and esoteric research).

We still operate in a vacuum that caters to traditional middle-class tastes, far removed in time and space from the problem areas of our society. We may not be as much a "part of the problem" as some other institutions, but neither are we a significant "part of the solution."

In practical, operating terms our irrelevance and our poverty are complementing, reinforcing parts of a vicious circle. Dollar-starved management buys the cheap-jack and the jerry-built. This prevents environmental excellence. The resultant poor environmental base combined with thin-spread staff vitiates efforts to involve the public in park-based environmental ethic/action programs. This means continuing irrelevance and poverty . . . and on and on.

This descent towards oblivion will not be broken until political decision-makers are convinced that park and recreation resources are more, much more, than places to have a little fun or learn the names of butterflies and dead generals.

Park managers today, starting with current levels of money and staff, must somehow break the mold of irrelevance and parochialism by constructively working themselves and their resources into the crucibles of societal concern and conflict. By this means, having become "part of the solution," we become essential to society; and society (here meaning the political jurisdictions that allocate dollars) then gives us the wherewithal to expand our leadership role in environmental reform, which makes us ever more important and deserving on society's priority list.

The old management systems and practices feed upon themselves and the yellowing rave notices of more tranquil times—finally eating themselves out of business. New systems of advocacy and involvement-where-it-counts build upon themselves and upon society's current needs.

This is *the* basic strategy statement, combining all that has been said about environmental crisis, mission, commitment, goals. Most of what follows is a manual of tactics that shows how the park and recreation profession, employing dynamic environmental management, can drag itself, sometimes kicking and screaming, into these latter, decisive decades of the twentieth century.

On a more specific level, corollary factors that obstruct environmental management include:

The attitude among many managers that environmental management is just an overlay upon management-as-usual—something a bit faddish that gives lip-service to growing public awareness.

This attitude, self-defeating on the face of it, produces two bad results: First, it prevents real analysis of current destructive management practices because it avoids questioning the premises and systems whence those practices derive; second, it creates the illusion of two management systems—"regular" management and "environmental" management. Thus the latter becomes a bothersome added "program," to be downgraded when it interferes with getting regular work done.

Environmental management is the heart and substance of park and recreation management; they are one and the same thing. Once this premise is accepted, then those current management systems and practices that don't square with environmental management standards can be dropped or modified. When this begins to happen, environmental management ceases to be an additive and becomes instead *the* management substance in the park or recreation area.

The organizational inertia—based on previous non-environmental programming, planning, and design—that perpetuates destructive developments and programs.

The momentum of the obsolete and destructive sustains force because of historical heritage ("We've always done it this way") and because of the traditional view that an agency must spend, not turn back, appropriated funds. The environmental illogic of persisting with destructive facilities development, for example, is evidently less painful for most managers than reworking plans and designs (and the organizations that produce them). The pain of turning back money is twofold: First, such action might jeopardize the level of future appropriations; second, the appropriating body might get the idea that park managers don't know what they're doing.

But the manager who allows such short-term pains (or his anticipation of them) to inhibit corrective action is simply blinking at the destruction of the resource he is charged to protect. This kind of malfeasance will be discovered eventually, and the ensuing pain will be fatal.

Freeman Tilden's phrase "the virtue of inaction" (pending development of sound environmental management techniques) has got to be the rationale and the guide for park managers who would stop environmentally unsound practices and programs.

Finally, the historical missions and legal frames that limit management scope of action, produce agency and unit competition and cross-purpose, and compel non-environmental management practice.

Park and recreation resources must be more than

preserves for the rich and mobile. They must become environmental-reform laboratories for the whole population—places where environmental quality and human welfare come together for the benefit of all. Attitudes, laws, and traditions must change to allow this broadened scope of management action.

The non-integration of government-agency and -unit missions at all levels produces contradiction exemplified in the large by the perennial highway vs. parkland competition, in the small by the internal cross-purpose objectives of preservation vs. use (the park ecologist trying to save a fragile biota vs. the planner who advocates road access). Such contradictions are as often the fruit of ignorance and poor communications as they are the product of calculated competition. (This is not to say that realpolitik among competing agencies is dead!) Coordinating mechanisms must be devised at all levels to assure (a) full evaluation of environmental cost/benefit ratios for different types of resource use, and (b) environmentally sound tradeoffs based thereon.

Often, particularly in new recreation areas and parks, authorizing legislation contains politically dictated seeds of environmental disaster (e.g., roads, schools, libraries, and other promised developments where they shouldn't be; or grazing, mining, and industrial provisions). Park and recreation managers, if they fail to avert such traps during the legislative process, must learn to cultivate public support aimed at rectifying mistaken laws. The old notion, "If that's what the law says, we've got to live with it," is a dodo-bird attitude. Laws can be changed when the public sees the need for doing so—which implies an aggressive, politicized management that can drum up public support and action.

A few examples will help tie down the meaning of environmental mis-management. These examples range from national scope to very particular instances within a given park or recreation area. But they are generalized to serve as analogs for any park or recreation area manager. After all, the same basic sequences apply in resource management, whatever the jurisdiction: setting of standards and objectives, then the programs, plans, designs, construction (or lack thereof), and operations-maintenance to meet those standards and carry out those objectives. Also, the same kinds of pressures, internal and external, operate in all jurisdictions to frustrate environmental management.

Let's start with the big picture. The first example is inter-regional geographically, but national in the scope of political, economic, and social factors involved. It shows the strength of the interlocked patterns that push our entire society toward environmental destruction. It reveals the links that bind business, industry, and government agencies to a course of ecologic, esthetic, and social disaster. It is a commentary on how weak a countervailing force is today's park and recreation complex when confronted by the Super Growth syndrome still dominant in our society. By way of analog, state and local park managers can substitute state or local agencies, chambers of commerce, and industries to make this example apply to their operating context.

Chapter I cited the trend of ever-expanding electric power production (as opposed to an ecologically determined power budget) as the basic symptom of our society's unwillingness to face environmental imperatives. In the Far Southwest this subject is more than academic. Being built there is a system of six huge coal-fired power plants. They will have clobbering impact upon the Nation's scenic heartland and the people who live and visit there. At the time of this writing one of the plants operates at a 2,075 megawatt capacity near Farmington, New Mexico. Daily it spews out hundreds of tons of fly ash and invisible poisonous gasses. Aerial tracking of visible air pollution shows that this one plant soils air, water, land, and people over an area of 100,000 square miles in the Four Corners area of New Mexico, Arizona, Utah, and Colorado. Based on observed effects of the Farmington plant and the climatology of the region, scientists of Los Alamos Scientific Laboratory predict that the fully operating plant system (14,000 megawatt capacity) will produce the noxious smear of an industrial environment from Southern California to the Rocky Mountains.[2] It simply means goodby to the distances and spaces and mountain ranges floating over the plateaus and canyons of this great country. Already photographers and artists note the smoggy degradation of Grand Canyon caused by the Farmington plant.

Beyond esthetics rear spectres of poisoned air, thermally-polluted and salt-concentrated water, and the great physical and cultural dislocations caused by strip mines, transmission lines, and other support and distribution tentacles of the industrial octopus. The power will go to Los Angeles, Phoenix-Tucson, and Las Vegas, there to encourage more megalopolis—more mistakes to burden the future.

The National Park Service began to sense the magnitude of looming disaster in the summer of 1969. It questioned the effects of the power-plant system on its chain of Colorado River parks and recreation areas from Canyonlands to Lake Mead, on the Navajo Land group of Arizona and New Mexico, on the Zion-Bryce complex in southern Utah, on Mesa Verde in Colorado.

Significantly, the National Park Service was not a party to planning councils until it forced itself in. But by that time basic commitments between the Bureau of Reclamation (the lead federal agency in the project) and the utilities consortium were already signed, sealed, and delivered.

Grasping at straws, the Service's Southwest regional office proposed a halt on further development of the plant system, pending an independent scientific evaluation of potential environmental effects. But the momen-

---

[2]See Albuquerque *Journal* series on power plants, July-August, 1970.

tum of commitments, contracts, and political pressures was too great. In effect, the concrete had already been poured. At this time it appears that only non-governmental pressures can halt or modify the power plant project. Unless they do, the magnificent park and recreation lands of the Far Southwest will disappear under a poisonous pall that will make mockery of the Nation's intent to preserve and enjoy them.

What are the lessons to be learned from this environmental management failure? Most obvious is the fact that the National Park Service defaulted as a dynamic environmental manager. Its conceptually sound proposal for scientific evaluation before further development speaks well of good intent. But the Service was intimidated by Interior Department protocols and politics (both the Service and the Bureau of Reclamation are Interior agencies; the Secretary of the Interior signed the Colorado River water-use contracts and approved others dealing with coal mining and water-use on Indian lands). So its efforts were timid, and, as the result shows, impotent. For example, higher echelons of the Interior Department learned of the proposal for independent scientific evaluation only through the prodding of non-governmental conservation groups—two months *after* the proposal arrived in Washington. Given the stakes—the ecologic health and esthetic preservation of the Southwest's prime park and recreation lands—this was something less than fearless defense of its resources by the responsible agency.

The Service failed again by remaining ignorant—until too late—of regional plans that could not help but jeopardize the integrity of its areas. This failure stems from two causes: bureau and boundary blinders (my bureau, my boundary is the limit of my concern); and Bureau of Reclamation procedures that effectively excluded a vitally concerned sister agency from planning councils at the formative stage of the project.

These strictures are not meant as petty fault-finding, nor are they directed at individuals caught in the mesh of custom and departmental protocol. Rather, they are stated to illustrate forcefully how hopelessly obsolete are these modes of operation and their underlying management systems. This environmental management default derived preeminently from a systems failure, marked by the symptoms of poor communication, cross-purpose, and contradictory result. All of which proves the need for a politically potent environmental coordinating agency that can police the affairs of competing departments and agencies, thus forcing compliance with the intent of the National Environmental Policy Act of 1969—whose spirit is grossly violated by the power plant project. Without such an ombudsman agency—accessible through both government and private channels—the destructive patterns of historical agency missions and interest politics will persist. Hopefully, the new Environmental Protection Agency together with the President's Council on Environmental Quality (established by the Act of 1969) can force the new patterns needed to give environmental management a chance.

But park and recreation managers cannot wait for that millenium when each agency and each jurisdiction has its "the environment comes first" patron. If this profession doesn't boldly fight its environmental conservation battles *now*—despite the dead hand of old rules and tradition-bound hierarchies and politics—variations of the power plant project will be repeated over and over again, across the land, to the eternal pauperization of the future and our children.

The principles of failure and default derived from this example apply in every jurisdiction, whatever the scale or context. Is a city park to be converted to a parking lot? Is a county park to be cut up for an industrial plant? Is a state park to be grabbed for an Interstate highway exchange? In every case the same kinds of people are using the same kinds of argument to justify the same definition of progress. And no matter how local or how big the context, the weights and powers of destruction seem just as irresistable, and the fears of battle against them just as clutching.

Is it any wonder that park and recreation people, apolitical by tradition and temperament, good guys who want to be loved, haven't been the successful crusaders the times demand?

By way of final digression, let us use this broad-scope example of environmental *mis*-management to make explicit the breadth of scope of constructive environmental management.

Good agency intelligence in a terribly complex, accelerating world gives managers the factual basis to control and shape the future—as opposed to just letting it happen, then picking up the pieces. In this example, such intelligence was lacking, and the National Park Service got into the act too late. Simple liaison between agencies is not enough. There must be vigorous probing by professional staffs into the affairs of other agencies and other jurisdictions, public and private, to see what's coming. On the model of investment-firm forecasters, environmental managers must keep current on economic, industrial, and social trends if they would anticipate and avert threatening manifestations of those trends. In this example, the potential for power plant development was known long before the contracts were signed. Given this knowledge and the hardly secret fact that power plants are heavy polluters, the Park Service should have marshalled scientifically based arguments against their installation long before the Interior Department sanctioned their development. This should have happened *despite* the fact that administrative agreements and legislation contained provisions for such development. When laws or prior commitments are environmentally wrong, every effort should be made to change them!

Public involvement in such anticipatory blocking moves is essential. Thus the park and recreation agency does its duty by alerting the public it serves. Thus does the public get involved in basic environmental issues—at the level of questioning trends themselves. Certainly the matter of trends is fundamental in this example: Is the production of more power for Los Angeles worth significant degradation, even destruction, of the Southwest's scenic heartland—a *national* resource? If not, what are the alternatives to the proposed power plants (such as a power budget)? Once this question sinks in, the public begins to face *the* fundamental environmental issues that must be faced—soon. Any environmental action/communication effort that doesn't get finally to this base level is fluff.

It cannot be escaped that environmental management to perpetuate the Nation's park and recreation lands provides the action crucible for public involvement in the larger across-the-land environmental reform movement. Didactic programs on environmental virtue and good sense (formal lectures, films, guided tours, school outings) can help to establish general acceptance of an environmental ethic. But only if the public sees the Nation's park and recreation lands as the first line of defense against *general* environmental decay; gets involved at the action level to save them; and begins to see the local, regional, and national implications in such saving (e.g., how many institutions and individuals are passengers on the power plant juggernaut?)—only then will environmental communications begin to mean something. The statement that park and recreation lands are the first line of defense against general environmental decay deserves analysis: It is just because environmental quality is so finely balanced that quality environments are so vulnerable. It is just because the struggle for life in degraded urban environments is so hard that park and recreation areas tend toward expendability, particularly when they are irrelevant to the social stresses in urban areas. Thus great cities—desperate to ease their own pain and squalor—reach out to the hinterlands for more power. Their political weight is irresistable. In getting the power they degrade the hinterlands. After all, what is more important—millions of urban dwellers who need air conditioning, electric heating, and pop-top aluminum beer cans, or a few birdwatchers in the boondocks? This is the framework of power relationships that confronts the environmental reform movement.

In this light, saving the park and recreation resources of the Far Southwest means these kinds of things: (a) preserving regional environmental integrity, because quality park and recreation environments cannot exist in a context of surrounding, boundary-violating degradation; which means (b) challenging and beating the established political and economic powers that want the power plants (an interlock that includes New York investment houses, governments, businesses, industries, farmers, Indians, etc.); which means (c) coming up with alternatives to unrestrained urban growth and per capita consumption of electricity; which means (d) ecologically determined modification of economic and social systems, including redistribution and regrouping of populations, decentralization of urban functions, and refinement of technology, community design, and communications to achieve fair man/man and symbiotic man/environment relationships. . . .

Now that's a pretty big order. But that's what stopping the power plants implies. That's why it makes sense to view park and recreation lands as the first line of defense against general environmental decay. *Because*, to save them, society must save the total environment, that is, society must save itself.

The sooner the public gets involved at the action level in such fundamental struggles, the sooner it will begin to understand the magnitude of the task ahead. Until we of this profession learn the trade of environmental action/communication by sparking such public involvement, the rest is good-intentioned futility.

It's almost tempting to stop here. Having glimpsed the import of total systems failure, the futility of trying to pin blame on any place or on any one, the dispersion of decision, the glacial movement by small increments toward an unknown but foreboding future—well, what the hell, I, you, we can't do anything about *that*.

But this sort of comforting despair doesn't solve any problems. In fact it kills motivation for energetic reform. And it overlooks some handles reformers can use.

Increments and decision points are those handles. Each increment in an evolving scenario is a link in the chain of events. It must be forged before the next link can be fitted on. If a link is held off by an individual manager (i.e., decision maker), the sequence is held up.

Most mature organizations have learned how to avoid positive decision making. That way no one decision maker can be isolated and held accountable. Rather, the organization sets a general objective, turns loose its technicians who contribute data and plans; then a solution machine (a committee) fits the pieces together into a jigsaw puzzle called "the project" or "the program." In this process, nobody has made a positive decision. The committee savored delusions of decision-making when it whittled on the data and plans (from diverse, non-integrated technical pigeon-holes) so that they would fit reasonably well into the puzzle. But such whittling is merely a mechanical process that avoids decision on the puzzle itself. Even the approving authority didn't make a decision. He merely ratified the work of technicians and whittlers, whose expertise he neither shares nor has time to question.

Out of this process comes a package of plans, money, and people who implement the project or program. They avoid decision too, because theirs not to reason why; theirs but to translate the plan, as drawn, into some sort of reality: a road, a building, an interpretive program. At work at this stage is the assumption that "Those guys up there surely knew what they were doing when they drew up this plan . . . to fill up the Grand Canyon. . . ."

This all leads to the notion that negative decision making (lacking means for positive decision) may be the key to environmental reform—pending reform of management systems to make them positive-decision systems. By being negative and obstructive in the face of an environmentally destructive project or program, a manager can frustrate the chain of events. He can grab a strategic link (one of the increments) and hold on to it, thus halting the whole misbegotten mess.

Of course he has to take the consequences. Organizations favor people who find their being in the organization. Thus if the organization says "You're a good guy," then you're a good guy. If it says "You're a bad guy," then you're a bad guy. This means that people are non-persons until the organization tells them who they are. Now, under these circumstances, the worst thing a guy can do is be negative and obstructive.

But there's another way to look at this. The manager (the bureau, the work unit, the technician) who goes along with disaster to avoid being negative and obstructive is going to get his after all. Because someday his boss is going to find out or be called on the carpet about the disaster, and then he'll say, "Why didn't you stop that mess?" Then who's the good guy and who's the bad guy?

For the next example of environmental mis-management we shift to a smaller frame: contradiction and cross-purpose within a single organization. It takes us to a major western park, and to a road that scars it. Some 30 years ago the park was smaller than it is now. To get the land needed to round out the boundaries, the park agency made a deal with the local populace: It would build a cross-park scenic road to benefit business in towns at the road termini. Thus condemnation proceedings (which can bring on small wars in those parts) were averted, and the park got a pig in a poke.

The terrain that the road would cross is rugged— deep canyons filled with rushing streams, overlooked by ridges and backdrop mountains. A comprehensive road alignment study during World War II recommended that the road run the ridges for maximum scenic benefits, and to avoid destroying the canyon-bottom streams.

What with the Korean War and economic troubles, getting money to build the road proved difficult, and the years passed by. The early road study got filed. But the commitment to build the road endured.

After the war, renewed local pressure and easier money combined to revive the road project. A new planning team came to the park with directions to turn out a plan. Spread thin by other projects, the team spent inadequate time on the ground aligning the road. The years of limbo between the first planning effort and the second one had broken administrative continuity. So the old plan, and its environmentally sound rationale for ridge-running, did not influence later deliberations but remained unused in the files. The second-round planners put the road in a canyon, with grades rising to highpoint overlooks. The plan was approved.

During construction, which was contracted out, park agency inspectors warned that the road alignment and poor supervision were producing disaster. They proposed a stop order that would give time to restudy the road. But the commitment-based momentum of the project, the razor-thin margin of construction money (which would be overdrawn by costly halts and change orders), and divided authority within the park agency combined to frustrate the inspectors' stop-order recommendation.

The road is built now. And, as feared by the inspectors, it is an esthetic, ecologic, and engineering catastrophe. Huge cuts and fills on side-hill grades destroy the canyon scenery. In engineering parlance, the angles of repose of these cuts and fills are too steep for the unstable geologic formations the road crosses. Washouts and massive slumps of rock and mud periodically close the road and dam the stream, whose course and ecology have been rudely altered by the encroaching road. Clearing the road after these mishaps and trying to avert them by emergency stabilization drain the park maintenance budget.

Belatedly, new studies are commissioned to straighten out the mess. But even if the engineering problems can be solved, which is uncertain, the esthetic and ecologic mayhem cannot be undone.

What are the mistakes and the lessons from this example?

First: The danger of politically forced tradeoffs ("We'll build the road you want if you'll sell the land"). Always questionable because they come back to haunt future managers, such deals should be shunned like the plague; they should be made only for an overriding gain. Hard negotiations, even condemnation, are not too great a price if they avert disaster for future managers—and, more important, if they protect lands in which the whole populace holds principal interest. Unfortunately, it is always tempting to burden the future in exchange for an easier, less painful today.

Second: The administrative discontinuity that buried the old plan and put the time-pressed second-round planners at great disadvantage. Instant planning itself is a major cause of environmental mis-management. When combined with ignorance of previous studies and older files (sometimes lost in indiscriminate record disposal programs), it robs managers of valuable data and produces mistakes.

Third: Inadequate funding for environmental protection. *All* projects that have potentially significant effects on the basic resource should have budgeted a *large* environmental protection contingency. Experienced programmers recommend a built-in 30 percent lump sum. This would allow stop orders and change orders so that unforeseen on-the-ground problems can be tackled sensibly—not just bulldozed through, to the ulcerated dismay of the managers and maintenancemen who get the booby prize.

Fourth: Inadequate plan-and-design review. Most managers can't or don't have time to make head or tails out of road profiles and other technical drawings. On-site reviews backed by veriform models are minimum necessities for translating plans and designs into realities that managers can truly decide on.

Fifth: Poor construction supervision. On major construction projects, most of which are contracted to private companies, agency inspection personnel should not only be competent to spot and challenge contractor short-cuts and malfeasance; they must also have the status and prerogative with the contractor and within their own agency to control the situation.

Sixth: Divided authority that paralyzed managers and technicians, preventing them from stopping what they knew was wrong. The complex work-unit relationships and divisions of labor that make organizations efficient can also produce gross inefficiency. There must always be hot-line, channel-bypassing procedures and communications that allow managers to stop instantly the rape of their resource—whatever the dispersion of technical and organizational authority. All of which won't mean a thing unless managers are smart enough and gutsy enough to use them.

In sum, this example shows how intra-agency dispersion of authority and technical expertise can create chaos. It points again to the need within the agency for a coordinating, environmental ombudsman who, in the first instance, would have rejected the faulty plan, and, in the second, would have cut through the administrative mesh to stop the faulty construction. Finally, the park manager and upper echelon managers abdicated responsibility by throwing it to engineers, planners, designers, and project supervisors. No matter the organizational obstructions, no matter the mythology of expertise, responsible managers should have bombed the project by going to the top, once the outlines of disaster became apparent. Better to have an unfinished abortion than a finished monster, which is a variation on "the virtue of inaction."

Two more examples take us into the park or recreation area itself. They show how lack of coordination, even of rudimentary communication, between operating units can foul things up.

In a desert park, the ranger, in his wildlife management guise, decided to increase wildlife watering places. The superintendent approved a plan to divert water from a natural, spring-fed drainage into a dry wash about a mile away. The maintenance unit installed a valve in a diversion pipeline that was part of an emergency water-supply system for a developed area. Unless the water in the pipeline was being pumped to the developed area (which happened rarely) the special valve was opened, diverting the flow from the spring into the formerly dry wash. One day the park naturalist came across the now-flowing wash. He walked to its head and discovered the open valve in the pipeline. Then he trekked to the spring-fed drainage channel where an ecologically important desert-stream biota was just about dead from drought. Upon the naturalist's urging, the diversion was stopped and now plants in the natural drainage are recovering.

In another desert area, a new trail was built through a fine stand of cactus. Later an agency ecologist discovered the trail, walked it, and found that it traversed one of the area's oldest, most important research plots—a pristine place set aside to serve as a biotic benchmark. The trail construction ruined it.

Mistakes? Lessons? In both instances, single-line objectives—not necessarily bad in themselves—produced implementing action destructive of critically important resources. That these projects could be carried to completion before the biologists discovered them testifies to the state of non-coordination and non-communication in the two areas. In the last example, a research-plot map for the area existed. But only the ecologist knew where it was filed. In operational terms, the map didn't exist.

These examples show how important it is that every environment-changing proposal be subjected to inter-disciplinary evaluation. The manager who doesn't provide the mechanism for and the enforcement of this most rudimentary environmental management technique (i.e., the manager who doesn't effectively use his staff talent) invites pigeon-hole projects that end up as problems.

¶ This chapter has emphasized natural regions, areas, and enclaves. The rationale for this emphasis is the fact that we must finally go back to healthy natural entities to get instructions for building healthy social entities— entities that interact constructively and symbiotically with the rest of nature.

Yet this stated emphasis is illusory. For in every instance the causes of environmental mis-management, and subsequent breakdown of natural processes, have been traced to social-process (organizational and inter-personal) failures. There could be no stronger vindication of Dr. Smith's statement, which introduced this chapter: "Environmental quality and human welfare are not two independent evaluations. They are two views of the same system of interactions."

On that note let us explore more explicitly the meaning and potential of environmental management in the historical, recreation, and social dimensions. In areas, properties, or enclaves stressing these dimensions of visitor experience, the natural fabric typically has been severely altered by man's activities, historical or modern. Environmental management of such areas is not dedicated to conserving pristine nature. Rather it aims to *illustrate* or *facilitate* human activity.

An historical area, for example, may show how man/man relationships led to success or failure in man/environment relationships. A battlefield could show failures. An ancient culture site might show balanced adaptation. An 18th-century garden could illustrate man/environment amenities. A site commemorating a scientific or technologic event could show the significance of that event in subsequent man/man and man/environment relationships. In every instance, management of the physical resource is a means to an end: communicating a history of man in the environment. Thus environmental efforts in historical areas, once the imperatives of historical integrity are met (preservation, authenticity), center on imaginative environmental interpretation and education.

A recreation area facilitates current human activity, both physical and social. Here the environmental manager blends natural and social processes to produce a pleasant physical environment—a setting for pleasant experiences in the recreation/social dimensions. Thus the natural dimension complements but is subordinate to the other dimensions, where environmental management's thrust might be either physical recreation or social reconstruction.

In sum: Environmental management definitions and objectives in areas that stress historical, recreation, and social dimensions differ functionally from those in natural-dimension areas. But environmental integrity (the proper blending of natural processes with historical and social processes) is just as hard to come by; and once achieved, that integrity is just as hard to hang on to. Here environmental management comes full circle, for the same destructive forces threaten *any* quality environment, whichever dimension it represents; and the same brand of public-arousal environmental management is required to save it.

Environmental management spans the four dimensions in other ways: For example, an urban planner might immerse himself in the natural dimension to experience quietude, solitude, and natural esthetics. Then he might visit an urban historic site that illustrates how men of the 18th century planned and built their cities so that quietude, solitude, and natural esthetics could be part of the urban scene. Then, in his environmental reform work with a neighborhood action group, he could combine these insights in a plan for the neighborhood that would provide settings where modern urbanites could experience quietude, solitude, and natural esthetics.

This interlude on environmental management in the "other" dimensions can well conclude with the fifth example of environmental mis-management: We go to a city ghetto where a system of neighborhood vest-pocket parks is being developed. Unfortunately, the planners and managers of the project are middle-class whites who don't take the time and trouble to find out what the black people of the ghetto want. So they build typical pre-ghetto-period urban parks—a few trees, plots of grass and flowers, maybe a statue or a fountain. These little jewels of manicured greenery, laid down in sick neighborhoods, just don't fit. Neither in appearance nor in function do they requite the needs of the people who are supposed to use them. "That's a whitey statue!" "Keep off the grass my ***!" The insensitive, irrelevant intrusions arouse anger, and the parks get vandalized beyond redemption.

This example sets the scene for later discourse on environmental management in city park and recreation areas. Basically, the ghetto setting demands a most sensitive *human ecology* viewpoint. Environmental management here must take account of value-system differences produced by the deprivations of ghetto life. And it must be directly relevant—in the daily-life-and-work sense—to the present and backlog human needs of people aspiring to escape the traps of poverty and humiliation. Not an imported big-sky man who knows best, but the people themselves must define those needs and the means to requite them.

¶ Environmental management begins when the park or recreation manager accepts the environmental imperative and his mission as environmental reformer.

Next the manager looks at his organizational, jurisdictional, geographic, zone-of-influence context of operations. Who are the people that I report to, am responsible to in the organizational and political sense? Which of them would be amenable to my expanded mission, which would reject it? How do I get my proposals to patrons, avoid deadends?

What are the laws and regulations that define my operational scope now? Which of these invite, which impede, broad-scope environmental management? Can I fashion a charter from existing authorities, or must I get a new charter?

Where am I in this country? What are the major (strategic, multiplier-effect) physical-human environmental problems in my region, state, county, town? How can my resource be used as an exemplar and base for environmental reform, relating as directly as possible to the environmental problems within my geographic zone of influence?

Who are the people whom I serve? Who should I be serving? How do I find out what they want and need?

These questions deserve the best answers attainable

by the manager, informed by the best contributions of his staff, his patrons, consultants, and clientele.

Having answered them, the manager and his staff prepare opening-wedge proposals for environmental management action—action that comprehends and involves his staff, his resource, his clientele, and geographic context.

The proposals strike for the immediately attainable, but they forecast a growing scope of action supported by a conceptual design for the future—itself supported by requests for new authorities, more money, more staff, as necessary.

Next the manager pushes the proposals through the organizational mill—using with discretion the supportive testimonials of friends in and out of the organization. And finally, he implements the proposals that survive.

In other words, in light of a new mission and new goals, the manager juggles current authorities, priorities, and personnel-dollar resources to build an environmental management foundation. Then he builds upon that foundation to complete the conceptual design for the future.

Preparation of environmental management proposals forces the manager to discover and state principles and standards of environmental management adaptable to his operational context. But there is a common environmental management core underpinning all operational variations. Abstracting from all that has gone before, here is an attempt to state the fundamental precepts of environmental management.

■*Environmental management is holistic.* It embraces all management functions and operations, all park and recreation personnel, all resource plans, activities, and uses.

■ *Management objectives must harmonize with environmental imperatives.* These imperatives occupy a spectrum whose end-points are *natural processes* and *social processes*. Depending on the setting and type of park or recreation resource—which will help define its best use in the environmental reform movement—management objectives may stress perpetuation of natural processes, preservation of an historical milieu, facilities for physical or esthetic recreation, or renaissance of social processes.

These management emphases do not conflict when the spectrum is viewed as a graphic analog of the total environment: Natural benchmarks provide visions of and standards for an ecologically healthy future. Historic sites preserve physical expressions of alternate value systems—places to compare the varied society-in-nature combinations evolved by other cultures and eras. Recreation areas allow the whole and healthy being in each of us to reach sunlight, to aspire to quality life. Social-process laboratories help people to replace individual misery and disorganization with community hope and direction.

Lacking the full spectrum, there can be no man/nature cohesion, no social cohesion. Lacking these forms of cohesion, there can be no philosophy to guide environmental reform, no community of interest and motivation to sustain men in the hard labors of environmental reform. Undergirding the entire spectrum, transcending the various emphases upon natural and social processes, the basic environmental imperative is affirmation of life as against destruction and maiming of life.

■ *Management objectives at the end-points of the spectrum are qualitatively different: When management emphasis is upon natural processes, objective data set the tone for development and operations. When management emphasis is upon social processes, subjective data set the tone.* One the one hand, the limits of the natural fabric, scientifically defined, guide the manager. On the other, he accommodates to, seeks guidance from, the people he is trying to involve in the social process. In both events preconceptions are dangerous.

■ *Environmental management avoids preemption of future choice.* Particularly in regard to manipulation of the physical environment, plans and developments should hold open all possible options for future resource managers. This concept is consistent with the notion of dynamic environmental management, evolving to meet the changing needs of an evolving society. The worst preemptions are those based on inadequate resource knowledge and pinch-penny development funding.

■ *Environmental management cannot wait upon the last research datum.* Most of the gross errors of environmental mismanagement stem from two management failings: not using fully the data and staff talents at hand, the proceeding with physical developments in ignorance. Lacking time or the resources to assemble special research talent, the environmental manager allows those projects that square with the best at-hand data and staff advice, disallows projects where more research is obviously needed. In both events, positive decisions are in order — on the one hand based on the existence of data, on the other based on the absence of data.

■ *Environmental managers create the organizational climate and the mechanisms that assure interdisciplinary debate of all management proposals.* The climate dissolves such human failings as professional jealousy and false pride. The mechanisms force the cross-checking between disciplines and work units that produces coordinated, predictable results.

■ *Environmental management synthesizes in-boundary and out-boundary concerns, in a regional frame, through public involvement in the setting of in-boundary and out-boundary management objectives.* Though planners tend to object to public participation (it is inefficient and upsets tidy systems), the greater inefficiency of irrelevance in a non-compatible context is worse by far. If the public does not have a real stake in the park or recreation area, it will not exert itself on the area's behalf to protect and make complementary its surrounding context.

From these generalizations certain specifics of physical-resource management emerge. These can be viewed as sample environmental management standards, i.e., the kinds of evaluation tools that allow us to judge actual management results against management aspirations.

Thus, any plan, project proposal, work order, working drawing, or contract that does not *automatically* — by its terms, materials, and resource allocations — protect the environmental integrity of the site to be worked on is faulty.

Thus, a project supervisor, maintenance man, architect, engineer, or any other person whose work or direction of work alters the physical resource must subject his way of doing the work to the imperatives of ecology and esthetics. If he doesn't, he is simply unprofessional.

Thus, a planner or designer or builder who lacks ecologic basic data can destroy a valley or a stream or a rare habitat without even knowing that he is doing so — or he can build a structure that violates geology or climate and becomes a maintenance rat-hole.

These examples point to the need for constant training and education of people in the organization. Managers must direct people to get this training and education. But every employee must be self-motivated as well *because* it is professionally necessary and morally right that he be environmentally sensitive to his work — whether that work is planning a park, cleaning restrooms, or deciding budget priorities.

The basic truth keeps surfacing: Environmental management is a total net, no one phase operating independently of the others. What the visitor experiences in the park or recreation area is the *combined product* of basic data studies, management objectives, programs, plans, designs, construction, and operations-maintenance. This means that environmental imperatives must be internalized throughout the organization so that they become the basic substance of all management processes and actions.

Visitor experiences include impressions of the area's surrounding context, the physical environment of the area itself, and the human environment of personal services and communications. The *quality* of these *visitor experiences* is the final judgment on the success or failure of environmental management. Only when we can show by the ecologic and esthetic health of our areas that we are professional, practicing environmentalists can we authentically communicate the environmental ethic to visitors.

This brings up a definition of *communication*. The term reaches beyond specific interpretive and educational programs to include the realm of silent language. Thus the condition of the restroom speaks an environmental message. So does the appearance of a road or a trail. The morale and proficiency of area personnel convey a message. The enforcement of environmental standards and the protection of park values say things. The concessionnaire's physical plant and operations speak volumes. Who then is not saying things to the visitor, verbal or non-verbal? And which of these messages is not ultimately environmental in basic substance? Total environment is total. It means all of us and the resource that we interact with. And the whole that comes through to the visitor is an environmental statement.

To conclude this chapter with some sense of pulling the strings together, I have chosen the scenario method to illustrate environmental management in àction. The five scenarios that follow touch upon these key elements of environmental management: (1) public involvement through environmental action/communication, (2) organizational coordination for environmental planning and development, (3) area-based environmental management techniques, (4) the public relations of imposing public-use limitations, and (5) the human ecology of ghetto-based park and recreation operations.

Scenario 1.

We go to a recently established reservoir recreation area in a western state. Authorizing legislation provided minimal, non-ecologic boundaries, i.e., a shoreline that fails to insulate the reservoir from the surrounding watershed, which is heavily impacted by industrial and grazing uses. These industrial (oil and gas) and grazing activities also occur within the boundaries, as provided in the legislation.

Incremental pollution occurs now, and there is the possibility of catastrophic pollution. The administering recreation agency defines the problem as degradation, possible destruction, of a recreation resource. A co-administering regional water authority fears pollution because it means bad water for the municipalities and industries of the dependent water-use region. If the reservoir were critically polluted, those living and working in the dependent region would face evacuation of cities and towns, economic disaster, industrial relocation, etc.

A sub-problem in this part of the country is a lingering frontier attitude that cheers exploitation of the land and deeply distrusts governments and their minions.

Solving this set of problems requires these things:

- research to get scientifically valid data on the pollution threat and the means to avert it

- a public information program originated by a respected local institution (not the suspected bureaucrats) that tells the dependent region what it must do to safeguard its water supply

- implementing action to insulate the reservoir from the pollution threat by changing the authorization act itself or modifying its effects through local regulation.

The scenario concludes in this fashion: In partnership with the equally concerned water authority, the recreation agency approaches the dependent region's major university. After briefing key officials, the agency asks the university to take on the research task and spearhead the public information program. The university accepts the challenge, because its own survival, as a dependent water user, is at stake, and because this kind of public action pays dividends with alumni and patrons. These alumni and patrons, incidentally, are the influential elite of the dependent region — businessmen, industrialists, newspaper publishers, and so on. When recruited by the university, this aggregation of interests starts beating the drums to save the reservoir. For they, too, are totally dependent on the water supply. The general populace now becomes aware — through editorials, TV specials, and public forums — of its own survival stake in the reservoir. Thus the environmental reform coalition gets grass-roots support. The exploiting interests, until now secure in their power, must bow to the united majority of the dependent region. Legal action follows, the reservoir is properly insulated, the pollution threat is averted.

In terms of strategy, the recreation agency protected its recreation-area interest by transcending it — both geographically and politically. If its protection policy had been limited to recreation benefits — rather than expanded to the much more fundamental water-quality issue — it would have fought virtually alone in a hostile climate. Once it had involved the enlightened self-interest of the entire community of dependent water users, success was ordained. This is the kind of public-arousal, catalytic environmental management that results in environmental reform action.

Scenario 2.

We go to a newly established natural area. This is a fragile, benchmark natural environment. Typically, because of public pressures and internal pressures from diverse organizational units, new area plans are rushed to completion before the area reveals itself as an environmental entity — and then it's too late. Needed is a methodology whose first stage reveals the environmental entity, then, under the umbrella of environmental determinants, integrates management objectives, plans, programs, development, and operations-maintenance.[3]

In this scenario we mount an experiment that will lay the base for full-scope environmental management of the new area. Vehicle for this experiment is a multi-disciplinary planning team comprising the area staff, an ecologist, environmental specialists from other natural and social science disciplines, and professional planners. To assure public involvement, local scientific and planning talents help the team as consultants.

The functions of this team will be: *first*, to define the environmental determinants that tell us what we can

---

[3] Major proponents of this methodology-for-today are G. Angus Hills, Philip H. Lewis, Jr., and Ian McHarg. Despite differences of approach, a common bond unites them: They analyze and evaluate the natural and man-made resources comprising the physical environment *before* recommending any alterations of that environment. (See also *Three Approaches to Environmental Resource Analysis*, The Conservation Foundation, Washington, D.C., 1967).

and cannot do as managers of this fragile area; *second,* to derive from this core of objective facts, the range of management options that will use but not abuse the resource; *third,* to construct a general plan for development and visitor use that compatibly synthesizes the environmental determinants and the management options; *fourth,* to derive from this general plan specific environmental interpretation/education plans.

The upshot of this planning sequence will be an area whose development and operations will conform to, not violate, the environment that we are charged to protect. By starting *first* with the environmental determinants and deriving from them management directions, we will avoid environmental wounds and abuses that would plague managers ever after.

If we can succeed in this experiment, we can set a precedent for further planning and development — not only for new areas, but also for established areas where management-imposed wounds have occurred. In the latter places we can learn how to cordon off the wounded sectors and rehabilitate them.

In many jursidictions this grand enterprise will appear fanciful. Not so! Scale it down if necessary to exploit the full range of talent in your organization, in local colleges and universities, and in landscape architecture and planning firms. No locale in this country is so lacking in human resources that the substance of this environmental planning and design methodology cannot be practiced.

Scenario 3.

We go to a long-established historical area. The character of this area's physical environment has been pretty well set by previous management decisions. Operations-maintenance is now the principal business of management, along with continuous modification of the physical plant and facilities to meet new visitor pressures and design improvements.

The superintendent initiates environmental awareness training involving his entire staff, representing
administration, maintenance, protection, and interpretation. He stresses that environmental concerns are to be
the key influence on all management decisions in the
area. Plans, programs, developments, operations-
maintenance proposals must all be screened by the
entire staff before any work commences. Thus the full
weight of the staff's multi-disciplinary knowledge of the
area environment can be brought to bear on every
project. Carrying capacity, ecological impact, and esthetics are the baselines of decision.

The superintendent then establishes procedures to
assure day-to-day adherence to environmental management standards. Each morning, before staff members go
out on the job, they gather for coffee with the
superintendent. The atmosphere is informal. Work
proposals are presented by each staff member to the
group. A safety project here, a supply order there, a
road or trail repair job over here, a visitor-circulation
modification over there. The cross-checking begins:
"Yellow safety paint on the stairway of the historic
structure? No! That would violate historical integrity. It
would be esthetically bad. Let's work out another,
compatible means to assure safety." Thus the screening
proceeds.

Maintenance questions a plan from the design
office for a new drainage ditch. "It wouldn't work,"
says he, "because it doesn't take account of natural
cross drainages there. And it would intrude on the
historic scene. I have a better idea." This one is
important — the ecology, the esthetics, and the integrity
of the site could be bunged up by this plan, if
maintenance is right. And "somebody up there" has
already approved the plan! "Well, let's go out and look
it over," says the superintendent. So they go — the
whole staff. They walk the ground. They all chip in
their thoughts. Upshot: The superintendent decides

against the approved plan; he buys the maintenance alternative — somewhat refined by the suggestions of administration, protection, and interpretation. A problem is defined; now the superintendent will follow through to solution, aided by justifications and plans drawn up by his staff.

Next item . . . .

Protection asserts that the concessionnaire is not meeting food-service criteria stipulated in the contract. Administration pulls the contract from the file and the staff goes over its terms. Interpretation relates that during visitor contacts he has heard these same criticisms from visitors. "Okay, we've got a problem. What do we do about it?" Maintenance notes the high employee turnover in the concession operation. "The new employees don't know the ropes." Administration suggests a training program for these new employees, to be conducted jointly by the concessionnaire and the park staff. Assignments are made.

Next item . . . .

Scenario 4.

This time we go to a live one — the California state park system. There, the director of parks and recreation instituted a reservation system for overnight camping. The alternatives were to expand camping facilities until the beaches were gone, or to continue packing people in until a quality camping experience was impossible — with all the attendant problems of waiting lines, overflow, and visitor irritations.

The secret of the director's success was an intensive education and public relations program that first converted his staff, then was beamed to Californians by all media. The impact of the event was anticipated, and was backed up by an administrative system for handling reservations. Thus people knew what was coming, and why it was coming, and they knew whom to contact to get a reservation. As a result, Californians — not noted for docility — have accepted the system. A by-product of their adjustment to it is a seasonal stretch-out that is spreading visitor use over a longer span of months.

As remarkable as the careful preparation and execution of this reservation system is the guts it took to tackle it. All too often park and recreation managers let their resources get trampled while presiding over visitor frustration and disappointment — visitors who came for inspiration and enjoyment, but fell right into another elbow-swinging crowd.

The imposition of visitor-use limitations, more necessary every day if quality environments and life experiences are to survive, is always a risky, politically loaded business. But like so many other immediately painful things, the alternative to a little blood now is a massive hemorrhage later. In California, the reservation system has become an important management tool which protects both the park resources and the quality of visitor experience. Further, the California experiment shows that an honest confrontation with environmental reality, if shared intelligently with the public, can be an effective medium for general environmental reform.

Scenario 5.[4]

Once there was a neighborhood museum in a ghetto. The white people who founded this museum for the black folks thought that they would appreciate knowing about the natural world. So they put a micro-zoo in the museum, including some snakes, rabbits, and gerbils.

---

[4] I credit John Kinard, director, Anacostia Neighborhood Museum, Washington, D.C., with the background for this parable of our times.

One day the director of the museum found little boys feeding the rodents to the snakes. "Why are you doing this cruel thing to the gerbils," he asked.

"Because they are rats and we hate rats," said the boys.

"Well," said the museum director, "what's all this hate for rats about?"

"Because rats run wild in our houses, and bite our toes at night, and ruin our food — that's what it's about," said the boys.

"Then you are really more interested in rats than in snakes and rabbits and gerbils?"

"Yes, indeedy! In fact, we want to know how to get rid of rats."

So, the neighborhood museum sponsored an exhibit on rats: where they came from, how they carry disease, how they live and multiply in human communities, and what human communities must do to get rid of them. As a result the people of the neighborhood got together, and, on the basis of this knowledge, organized themselves to get rid of rats. The battle still goes on.

This example of environmental management in the social dimension pulls all the strings together. The questions we ask about relevance, about how to use our resources for environmental reform, about new kinds of management scope and environmental communication— all of the answers are epitomized here. Here, too, is the bridge that takes us to the topics of environmental interpretation and education. As this example shows, they are not really separate topics; rather, they are specialized extensions of environmental management.

interlude IV

counsels
of hope

Our society must change radically, but it cannot change meaning-
fully unless its *people* change.
To make them puppets of a different
order, as many so-called radicals
are prone to desire, is to betray
both them and the radical ideal.
We must try to radicalize the
American people as so many of us
have been recently radicalized —
not by pushing them up against
the wall, but by helping them to
regain the sense of power over
their destiny that should be their
birthright.

The New Democrat
June, 1970

When hope fails, apathy sets in. What good does it do to get people excited about environmental crisis, infused with environmental ethic, if they cannot translate their concern into action? Stimulation with no place to go turns to frustration.

In this context, environmental interpretation must be a triple-threat medium: to inform, to motivate, to activate. Basic to this progression is the creation of hope. Basic to hope is the belief that there will be a future worth living. Basic to this belief is faith in man's intelligence, expressed as his ability to understand and abide by environmental imperatives — that is, his ability to control himself.

Through environmental management of park and recreation areas we create samplers where quality life in both the ecological and social senses can be experienced. We show that men *can* control themselves. Environmental interpretation starts from this base — as a justification of faith, a message of hope. By extension and analogy it then converts the small-scale fact into the large-scale potential: "If *some* men can control themselves and perfect their social processes to achieve environmental quality — as has been done here — then perhaps *all* men can do so in this community, in this nation, in this world."

Finally, having informed and planted the seed of motivation, environmental interpretation facilitates action. It encourages answers to these questions: "What should be done?" "How do I get started?"

chapter IV

environmental interpretation

Interpretation, as it has evolved in our profession, means the complex of media and personnel that tells the story of a park or recreation area. Interpreters are specialists who tell the story with films, lectures, tours, publications, exhibits, and so on. The "story" of an area usually means the history of an event, a person, or a natural phenomenon.

In non-urban recreation areas, interpretation usually is subordinate to orientation, which informs people about what to see and do. In urban recreation areas, interpretation usually is subordinate to instruction, which helps people perfect skills in games, crafts, and the like. Libraries, museums, neighborhood centers, zoos, and aquariums conduct varied programs that combine interpretation, orientation, and instruction.

Now let us break away from these traditional terms and types of communication to get a fresh perspective on environmental interpretation.

Environmental interpretation is that body of communications, devices, and facilities that conveys environmental knowledge, stimulates discourse on environmental problems, and results in environmental reform.
Environmental interpretation starts with the park or recreation resource and the visitors who use it. But the basic objective of environmental interpretation — motivating the public to take environmental reform action — forces it to transcend the resource and its visitors.

Environmental interpretation appeals to the whole man — sensory, affective, logical: It uses sensory experience to involve people in their human and physical environments. It stresses the esthetics of environmental health: the objective beauty of varieties-in-harmony; the subjective satisfaction in patterns-of-understanding. It uses facts to show relationships.

For convenience, the types of environmental interpretation can be termed:

- story-line
- resource management
- clearinghouse
- forum
- community action.

Discussion of these types — their objectives, limitations, flexibilities, and techniques — will be the main job of this chapter. But first, a digression to show how the structure and technique of environmental interpretation reduces the risk factor at the same time that it encourages public probing of environmental problems.

In traditional terms, interpretation is a form of education. Its practitioners educate the public. The public comes to the park or recreation resource as an audience. It listens respectfully to the interpreter, who is an expert on his subject — usually an arcane pinch of history, anthropology, or natural history. This is a cozy, safe relationship. Few people get angry over the botanical mysteries of, say, sphagnum moss, though some might get upset about the evolutionary implications of paleontology, or the assertion that the North won the Civil War. But these are tested traps. Basically, you have to stretch pretty hard to get people angry when interpretation limits itself to passive description of events and processes.

Environmental interpretation is different. It not only informs, it motivates to action — sometimes it *is* action. Even at the informing level, it ceases to be innocent nature study or whitewashed history. It questions value systems, folk heroes, and conventional wisdom. If it doesn't, it's a waste of time.

Now, an educator with a point of view is all too easily labeled a propagandist. *To avoid the "propagandist" trap, the interpreter learns the techniques of provoking people to think and reach their own conclusions, rather than slamming them between the eyes with his conclusions.*

Provocation is what interpretation was always supposed to be. But it was too easy to be didactic — to just tell the story and be done with it. Now provocation becomes the basic tool of the interpreter. With it he can get people beyond the aspirin-tablet level to the surgical-scalpel level of environmental discourse. To do this the interpreter must change his view of himself — from lecturing oracle (whatever medium he happens to be using), to instigator of thought and communication. The setting for environmental communication ceases to be a bunch of discrete items to be described; rather it becomes a pool of stimuli and relationships that people plunge into, there to swim to their own stroke. This is true whatever the setting, be it nature tour, environmental forum, or community action center.

The environmental interpreter uses three approaches, taps three sources, to provoke public involvement in environmental discourse and reform action.

First, he uses the story-line, the physical environment, and the social-process potential of his park or recreation resource to involve the public with the resource itself. Emphasis here is on traditional interpretive programs. The interpreter plays the role of expert, guide, instructor. He "talks" to get the public started. Essentially, this is the old interpretive bottle, though its contents and provocational techniques are expanded to serve environmental reform ends.

Second, he facilitates public use of his resource as a clearinghouse for the exchange of environmental information. The emphasis here is on general environmental discourse through media and lecture programs, research, and reference service. The interpreter plays a role similar to that of a program chairman or a reference librarian. *Other* experts (via films, literature, and other media) "talk" to get the public started. This is a newer interpretive bottle, and its contents are new, too, combining imported expertise and public interpretation of it.

Third, he facilitates public use of his resource as a base for environmental reform action. The emphasis here is on public forums that lead to community action. The interpreter plays the role of host. The public "talks" to itself to get itself started on environmental reform. This, too, is a new interpretive bottle, with new contents that the public itself pours.

In terms of risk (i.e., risk reduction), this three-role description of the environmental interpreter is important. In the first role, because he is talking about his own resource, the interpreter starts from a base of prestige that allows him to call environmental insights and concerns pretty much as he sees them. He is the expert, and if people take exception he can show them, on the ground, what he means.

In the second and third roles, the interpreter gets off the hook. Who is he to argue with or defend Barry

Commoner, The National Audubon Society, or a Congressional committee on poverty? He just helps the eco-activist public to get these viewpoints in circulation. If somebody wants to argue a viewpoint, let him go to the source. And certainly, the interpreter as host is not responsible for the conclusions and action plans of a public forum. He simply performs a public service by providing a setting for the forum.

In this light, discretion in an environmental interpretation program is more a matter of structure and technique than of content. As long as the interpreter stands up there alone haranguing an audience he is vulnerable to every form of ignorance and bias. When he prophesies doom (if things don't change) the ignorant optimist retorts, "How do you know?" When he opposes the building of a dam or a pulp mill, the builder and the Chamber of Commerce go for his jugular, if his boss doesn't get there first. Most important, when he, with specialized knowledge of environmental degradation, questions generally accepted value systems and assumptions, he turns off the public that he so desperately wants to reach — so his knowledge and his passion go for naught.

By contrast, if the environmental interpretation program is so structured that the public does its own exploring, thinking, and concluding — the interpreter using his resource as catalyst and setting — then content can range the full span of public concern. Eco-activists will jump at the chance to use a park or recreation resource as a stage for environmental discourse and reform action. They will see to it that the larger public is exposed to controversial viewpoints. And the atmosphere of dialogue will sort out the truth.

Though he has shifted the burden of environmental interpretation onto the public itself, the interpreter is not passive in the clearinghouse/forum setting. By creating that setting, by encouraging people to use it, he performs positive service. Further, he counsels and moderates and helps get answers for people with questions. To the extent that he himself seeks out valid data and authoritative experts to illuminate clearing-house/forum functions, he encourages factual accuracy, which helps to set a standard of reasoned discourse for the participating public. As this standard gains acceptance, the atmosphere of dialogue will prevail.

As asserted before, social cohesion is prerequisite to environmental reform action; bringing people together for reasoned discourse on common problems encourages social cohesion, discourages polarization and stridency. This in itself is a fundamental environmental reform — of man/man relationships. The interpreter is instrumental in this process.

The risks of environmental interpretation do not stop with the interpreter and the management that either sanctions his activities or stops them out of fear. Remember, the principal target of environmental interpretation is the business-as-usual syndrome that carries us all toward eco-disaster. It is the save-the-status-quo attitude that is threatened by environmental honesty and eco-activism. This is the fear that smothers reform elements of OEO's Community Action Programs. This is the resentment that gets activist ministers fired when they try to make the Gospel a call to humane reform, rather than a platitudinous salve for rich and poor alike. This is the complacency that commutes unseeing through the slums, then labels communistic and uppity the manifestations of slum discontent and despair. This is the interlock of interests, commitments, and priorities that fears ecology for what it is — the subversive science.

This is where the risk really is. *Because* environmental honesty and eco-activism might just get the public aroused enough to reject the outmoded philosophies and institutions that perpetuate the status quo of destruction.

Some people say that the "establishment" is too

blindly entrenched to be reformed by reason, persuasion, and peaceful political action. They say that to encourage belief in the efficacy of reform, to involve the people in reform programs, is futile and socially irresponsible. They say that such wasted motion only delays the moment of truth when the victimized public declares for itself through revolution.

Given the political simplistics, the environmental tokenism and fakery, and the Calvinistic morality (success means virtue; failure means vice) that signal a large part of the establishment's world view, the revolutionaries may be right.

But this book — reflecting the spirit of the Institutes — is based on different premises: that there is still time (if barely) for environmental reform, that our society can respond to that unifying need, that environmental interpretation can be one of the instruments leading to unified response.

This spirit assumes that men are savvy enough to assess magnitudes of risk. All particular perils — as seen by specific political, economic, or social groups of men — pale to insignificance before the ultimate one: an environment so degraded that the generality of mankind cannot survive. It is this transcendent peril, this equalizing threat, that gives environmental interpretation potential power. If we, in our particular groups, can be made to understand that we, as a species, either hang together or hang separately, then it makes sense to imagine dialogue among those who have heretofore cursed and suffered one another.

Environmental interpretation can help people to see today's ultimate peril — a biosphere being murdered; then provide settings where the antagonisms between groups can be aired — releasing the pressures; then encourage the atmosphere of dialogue in which groups can mobilize their mutual interests — to the end of environmental reform. In this process, the concept of risk changes qualitatively: from a destructive, divisive force to a constructive, cohesive force.

Environmental interpretation leads people to a basic question: What kind of a world do we want?

Environmental interpretation uses many modes of exploration and participation to acquaint people with environmental imperatives, and with the conditions of ecological and social health that would give humanity a shot at the good life — in all its geographic and cultural variations.

Environmental interpretation may demonstrate the mistakes that men have made. In this guise it may be a hard-line, "Thou shalt not . . ." kind of communication. At other times environmental interpretation may lead people onto pathways of sunshine and happiness, giving them a glimpse of the world that might be.

Environmental interpretation is a vast fabric of people, dimensions of experience, and types of resource, media, and technique. It can be dealt with here only in outline. Each type of environmental interpretation (story-line, resource management, clearinghouse, forum, community action) is loosely defined as a part of the fabric. Then its applications are illustrated by selected examples.

We start with story-line interpretation because that's where we have been. We already know something about it. This is the interpretation of nature hikes, historic sites, visitor centers, campfire programs, trail leaflets, roadside exhibits, and the like. It is subject-matter oriented, limited mainly to the natural and historical dimensions.

I start with the assumption that story-line interpretation has limited value in the environmental interpretation fabric. It is limited, first, because it must cater overwhelmingly to the casual visitor. The interpreter must work within the time-interest span of the mass of casual visitors. This means that he is restrained in developing the extensions, the analogs, the subtle webs of meaning that lift his park story above the literal and specific to the metaphoric and universal.

Moreover, most visitors come to natural and historical areas with their own set of expectations — to see a natural wonder; to stand in homage before a monument of history. In a general way they know what the place is about and what they want out of their visit. Any attempt by the interpreter to dilute, delay, or muddle the anticipated experience in the name of environmental pleading will be resented.

The scope of the story line itself, its suitability as a bearer of environmental tidings, may constitute a major limitation. It does no good to preach the whole environmental crisis from a limited story base, nor to leap from story line to anomalous conclusions. The strained, contrived interpretive pitch clangs with dissonance and does injustice to the park story.

Some limits we have imposed upon ourselves. I speak of the inertia of traditional interpretive techniques, facilities, and personnel. As today practiced, story-line interpretation is overwhelmingly taxonomic and passive-descriptive — names of things, narratives of no-context events. Most interpretive facilities date from the McGuffey era of interpretive-educational theory. And many interpreters function as walking textbooks whose microscopic erudition and canned lectures intimidate and turn off visitors.

Of course this grim portrait must be qualified. It does scant justice to many interesting technical innovations. It shocks many imaginative people whose best efforts are frustrated by interpretive programs that are obsolete and irrelevant. It is unfair to those exceptional interpreters whose initiative has produced new interpretive objectives and the programs to match them.

Environmental interpretation deals with relationships and processes (ecology), rather than items and names (taxonomy). But all too often old-style facilities (exhibits, AV programs, publications) trap interpretive programs and practitioners in gobs and gluts of detail. This problem is compounded when the interpreter, as interpreter, views himself as an academic scholar, rather than a skilled communicator of essential meanings — meanings whose context the interpreter builds in response to visitor needs and interests.

Now a final negative comment before crossing over to the sunny side of the street: In recent years many interpreters have sensed the irrelevance of their work. To work off frustration they have pursued far out electronic techniques, by-ways of antiquarianism or biological hair-splitting, and interpretive extravaganzas of all sorts. Many of these technically fine expressions contain no more substance than the hand-writ labels and photo racks they replaced. They may cost a lot; they may exhibit technical or scholarly virtuosity; they may be entertaining. But do they go to the heart of ecological and social concerns; do they edify; do they lead people to environmental ethic and reform?

This phenomenon of much action, movement, and technological flurry leading nowhere is typical of the whole society. Lacking unifying values and purposes, meaningless proliferations and variations at the technical level substitute for the important work that skilled and conscientious people really want to do. Maybe the values and purposes of environmental interpretation can help requite these deeper aspirations.

Turning from cavils and criticisms, it is time to get a positive fix on story-line interpretation.

The key to proper perspective is to view story-line interpretation as *one* form of environmental interpretation among many. Being aware of its limits and strengths, and of its relationships to other forms of environmental interpretation, the interpreter can exploit this form effectively — neither overworking it, nor neglecting it.

This perspective (one form among many) is *very* important. It spreads the interpretive load because it breaks the traditional boundaries of interpretation. So long as *story-line interpretation* and *interpretation* are synonyms — the traditional view — then the staff, subject matter, and modes of interpretation remain in a narrow rut:

Q. Who is concerned with interpretation?
A. The staff interpreter.

Q. What does he interpret?
A. History and natural history.

Q. How does he interpret them?
A. Slide-programs, publications, exhibits.

If we add to story-line the *other* forms of interpretation (resource management, clearinghouse, forum, community action), *interpretation* changes:

Q. Who is concerned with interpretation?
A. The entire staff . . . *because* every staff function and activity is an environmental statement, and is, therefore, interpretable;

and public involvement in environmental interpretation finds expression in the natural, historical, and recreation/social dimensions — and it ramifies throughout the physical and social environment of this resource and its surrounding context.

In this perspective, story-line interpretation can be viewed, first, as a part of the attraction that brings visitors to a park or recreation area, and, second, as the medium for transition to deeper levels of environmental understanding.

An example of this progression — from attraction to understanding via interpretive transition — is found in the summer evening bat-flight interpretive program at

Carlsbad Caverns National Park, New Mexico. (What follows is a hypothesized expansion of the present program; it's what *could* happen if all opportunities were grasped.)

The whirling, whirring cloud of bats circling out of the cave's entrance as dusk falls is a primordial natural phenomenon that triggers buried emotions and myths in the human soul. It is a world-famous spectacle that has attracted millions of people.

As the audience gathers each evening in anticipation of the flight, the interpreter provides context for the coming event: he describes the bats, where and how they live in the cave, why they fly out, where they go, and when they come back. *Here is story-line interpretation in its classic guise: explaining a natural or historical event for the enlightenment and enhanced enjoyment of the visiting public.*

But the interpreter doesn't stop there. He goes on to describe the alarming decrease of the bat population during the last few years — from tens of millions to only a few million. He briefly mentions scientific studies that tie the bat die-off to increased use of pesticides, which poison the insects that the bats eat, then concentrate in the bats' vital organs. He states that the bat flight will one day be only a memory if the poisoning doesn't stop. He breaks from this line of discourse by inviting interested visitors to meet with him after the flight for a special program on pesticide pollution.

A select part of the bat-flight audience accepts the invitation. They adjourn to an auditorium. The interpreter uses the fate of the Carlsbad bats to show why environmental management must go beyond the park boundary. He describes efforts by the park and its local supporting public to modify pesticide use in the Carlsbad farming region. He notes that business interests dependent on the tourist trade — and thus interested in perpetuating the bat flight—have set up public forums to hammer out a regional solution that benefits both businessmen and farmers. He states that the park hosts these meetings, inviting scientists from government agencies and universities to join them. The experts have come up with a valid action plan: reduce pesticides so that bats can live, because each bat eats hundreds of insects each night. It's a winner because the bat flight and pest control become mutually supporting elements of a natural solution.

Next the interpreter transcends the local context and shows a short film on worldwide pesticide pollution. He concludes the special interpretive program by recommending pertinent items from the park's environmental bookshelf, which displays publications that span the gamut of environmental crisis.

This example demonstrates all of the positive elements of the story-line form of environmental interpretation:

☐ Story-line interpretation reaches large numbers of people — all casual visitors with whom there is any interpretive contact, whether oral, written, or audio-visual.

☐ The interpreter has built into the story-line of the bat flight an environmental provocation directly relevant to the bat flight (it takes bats to have a bat flight) and to the experience of his audience (you are about to witness a dying phenomenon, unless . . .).

☐ The interpreter does not press the entire environmental crisis onto the unselected bat-flight audience. Instead, his story-line environmental provocation keeps within the context of the experience that the audience is about to have.

☐ Interpretive provocation and visitor experience are perfectly timed to reinforce one another. The visitor is living *now* the experience that is the barb on the interpreter's harpoon.

☐ Once the interpreter allows the special-interest

audience to *select itself*, he can, within reasonable limits, take off on environmental crisis with no holds barred. He is not frustrating visitor expectations — he is fulfilling them, for these are self-declared concerned people. Nor is he limited to point-for-point story-line interpretation.

☐ Having used the story-line as the transitional medium, he goes to the resource management form of environmental interpretation. He shows his select audience how environmental imperatives forced park management to go to the local public with the bat poison problem, and how this spreading of concern led to regional forums and community action.

☐ Finally, the initial story-line provocation allows the interpreter to involve his select audience in the clearinghouse function — an overview of environmental crisis using a film, publications, and discussion.

Note, too, in this example, how the problem of obsolete interpretive facilities is sidestepped (obsolescence may be of the technical or content varieties; or, most likely, both). Whatever the exhibits might be like in the visitor center museum, however inane the usual film program or the traditional sales publications — the interpreter operates independently of them. He selectively uses those facilities (auditorium, projector, bookshelf) that support *his* interpretive program.

The Carlsbad bats tie story-line interpretation directly to resource management interpretation, then on to clearinghouse, forum, and community action. The example is notable, too, because it shows two kinds of public involvement: first, a local public making the bats' cause its own, then going from understanding to action; and, second, a visitor public that can't be involved in the Carlsbad action, but whose specially interested members view the Carlsbad situation as spur and model for their own environmental reform action back home.

Often, story-line interpretation doesn't have this much punch and follow-through. It reaches most visitors at a level that informs them about ecology and the environmental ethic. But it lacks obvious ties to reform action. The interpreter is then challenged to make the specifics of his story-line serve as a window on the larger world of environmental crisis and reform. From his story-line he creates analogies and models that trigger visitor concern and response. The interpreter must be explicit when he uses Model A (his story-line) to illuminate Model B (the visitor's world), because educators hold little faith in the transfer of meaning from one universe of discourse to another, unless transition is made very clear.

Special resources, such as zoos, aquariums, and museums, are particularly adaptable to interpretation that helps visitors reach self-related environmental understanding — getting them from Model A to Model B. These resources are geographically and topically "free." A zoo or an aquarium exhibits animals from all over the world, from many life communities; a general museum can conduct environmental programs on any topic.

To show how the story-line world can be brought home to the visitor's world, let's go to a zoo. It exhibits many species of ungulates from Africa. Straight story-line interpretation has for years described the life history of these animals under ideal conditions. But that's the rub, and that's where the story-line goes hard-line environmental. In vast regions of Africa ideal conditions no longer exist. The habitats of these animals reflect the man/man relationships of the post-colonial world. Tribesmen, with growing numbers of cattle, compete for prime wildlife habitat. Poachers take their toll of wild animals. Predator-prey relationships disintegrate and the health of surviving ungulates declines. In our own country the fate of the bison shows what can happen — even to great herds thought inexhaustible —

when massive environmental assaults occur. Today we face serious problems in Alaska, where the fate of the caribou may be determined by oil exploitation in the barren lands. Even closer to home, deer and elk live in false environments (too small, too simplified) that force constant human intervention to avert nature's apocalyptic solutions to environmental imbalance. Thus does a zoo (museum) program on African ungulates circle the world, coming back to the visitor in terms of his own country and its ungulate management problems, which are seen as symptoms of more fundamental environmental disruption.

An aquarium might start out with whales — the fact that they are being hunted to extinction and that their once remote breeding grounds are being crowded by man. From the whale, and its man-caused problems, it is a short step to the endangered anadromous fishes — harvested to dangerously low population levels, then cut off from their spawning grounds by man's intervening dams and diversions. From the salmon, another short step gets the visitor to consideration of trout, which die as lakes and streams die. About then the interpreter mentions Trout Unlimited, a hard-nosed conservation outfit that minces no words in urging the basic reforms necessary to preserve a general environment that can support healthy surface waters where trout can live....

Museums, zoos, and aquariums multiply their influence as hard-line environmental interpreters through the public media, traveling exhibits, and publications. Examples include the televised programs of the San Diego Zoo; the truck-transported *Yellow Submarine* school exhibits of the Tennessee State Museum; and the American Museum of Natural History one hundredth anniversary exhibit and brochure, *Can Man Survive?* The last item is a classic illustration of hard-line environmental interpretation. It is a generalized story-line derived from the basic interpretative themes of the American Museum of Natural History. Striking directly at pollution, population, and human attitudes that threaten humanity, it means to unsettle people by making them face squarely the facts of environmental crisis.

Story-line environmental interpretation can be gentle, too, and in the natural dimension can be the invitation that helps a visitor become a belonging, knowledgeable, non-destructive part of a healthy environment. For example, the life community of a forest pond might be used as the window that reveals the underlying similarities of all life communities. A special folder or exhibit might introduce the visitor to the pond community, then give him clues on how to blend into and observe that community in action.

There must be such gentle moments. These are the times when a person senses the beauties and harmonies of nature — a general homeostasis whose parts are the lives and deaths of particular plants and animals. It takes times of belonging for people to feel veneration for the natural system that gave them life and sustains them in living. This non-sentimental love of earth, a kind of animism, reaches far back in human history and deep into individual consciousness. Unless people have opportunity to elicit these almost forgotten feelings in gentle communion with nature, they cannot learn to care for the natural system.

No matter the urgency of environmental crisis and the urgings of his own impatience, the interpreter must balance amenity and shock as instruments of environmental interpretation. Without belief in human and natural amenities people cannot care for men or for nature.

Man depicted only as despoiler, nature depicted only as despoiled, add up to disgust and fright. Environmental interpretation that presents only the negative, doom-saying side can badly skew visitor perception and response. Like the Delta children of Huxley's *Brave New World*, who were conditioned to hate flowers, visitors might be so negatively conditioned by shock-type negative interpretation that they could not devise positive man/man and man/environment relationships. This would be tragic irony — environmental interpretation destroying the hope and motivation that could fuel environmental reform.

Indeed, if environmental interpretation is to offer counsels of hope, it must help people fulfill "a biological and emotional need for an harmonious accord with nature."[1] René Dubos does not use these words lightly. As a biologist he looks at man as a species that evolved over millions of years. Genetically man is still a pretechnological animal. Social processes that insulate man from natural processes are inhuman and dehumanizing precisely because they deny the natural man in each of us.

The 1966 Conference on Man the Hunter at the University of Chicago explored this theme of schizoid modern man — technicized and urbanized on the surface, but biologically still barefoot in the boondocks. Perspectives developed in this conference suggest that the historical dimension is the key that can unlock the natural dimension. For 2 million years cultural man has been on earth; 99 percent of that time he has been a hunter-gatherer. Biologically modern man emerged some 50,000 years ago. In this perspective, the hunting way of life is the principal adaptation and shaping influence of species man. Our sensory, affective, and logical equipment is better suited to hunting a deer and gathering roots than it is to bearing the stresses of industrialized, urbanized society.[2]

This insight into the natural dimension by way of historical dimension suggests many themes for the environmental interpreter. For example prehistoric and historic sites can be interpreted in a thematic framework based on man's acquisition of technological power.

---

1 René Dubos, *So Human an Animal,* Charles Scribner's Sons, New York, 1968, p. 96.

2 R. B. Lee and I. Devore (eds.), *Man the Hunter,* Aldine Publishing Co., Chicago, 1968.

Translated into man's "conquest of nature," this power led to man's alienation from the natural world. The unifying simplicity of this theme — persuasively demonstrated in the book *Man and Nature*[3] — functions as a kind of lodestone, arranging the details of history into patterns of understanding.

At a direct, experiential level, the environmental interpreter can use this lodestone to help visitors get back into a pretechnological relationship with nature. What was it like, for instance, along the Camino del Diablo on the Arizona-Mexican border before modern amenities such as air conditioners and refrigerators and jeeps softened its rough edges? The following historical script[4] gets the visitor there intellectually. On-site realities of heat, wind, and dust get him there physically. Now he has a chance to actually feel what it was like when there was no escape from the natural world:

> The Organ Pipe Cactus region remained an anachronistic frontier until just yesterday. The essential conditions of life here were about the same for the rancher, miner, or outlaw of 1930 as they were for Father Kino three centuries before. These conditions were hard, little alleviated by the gaunt and strange beauty of the place. Because conditions were hard the human traffic was sparse. That traffic was made up mostly of men who were so busy at the hard scrabble of just keeping alive that they had little or no time to write about their struggle. They came here as missionary, frontier soldier, colonizer, traveler, surveyor, farmer, rancher, outlaw, miner, rustler, or Villista — they were defeated, and died or departed; or they won out, but only a few, and those few just barely managed to hang on. None of them wanted to talk much about it. A few were required to write a line or two in official reports. And in the latter days a few old timers — having finally gained a little respite — have reminisced. But even this last is a guarded business, because "the man so-and-so shot still has a son living in Ajo . . .."

So you come across an old stone cabin or a well shaft or a

---

3 R. A. and P. J. Watson, *Man and Nature,* Harcourt, Brace, New York, 1968.

4 Prepared by the author for Organ Pipe Cactus National Monument, Arizona.

mine and it has a name like Juan's Well. Who was Juan? When did he dig that well? Why? Nobody knows.

There is a lot of mute history here. It is marginal history because this was marginal country. Big events in the local context didn't make a ripple a hundred miles from here. A few big events passed through here, but they didn't stay long enough to get localized.

The history here is the sweating, grunting kind of history. It's 50 cubic yards of solid rock piled outside an empty hole on a mountain side. It's a deserted mesquite jacal with the wind whipping through, rattling a pile of rusty tin cans. It's a lean range cow peering into an empty well that someone dug 40 years ago. It's a rock grave on the Camino del Diablo.

But it is history, fully as important to the men who lived it as the more significant history — by conventional measure — that happened at Gettysburg or Independence Hall. It is a history of lonesome hopes, lonelier failure, small victories — in a land that gave only a little, and very grudgingly. It is a history of human ecology on an outback frontier. Despite local legend and repute it is rarely the individual that stands out here; rather, it is the breed of men that came here, many of them on life's last fling. It is the land itself that really dominates the story. Because the land is rugged, men chose predictable paths through its mountains. Because it is dry, they dug wells. Because its cover is sparse, they built houses of mud and cactus stems. Because its rocks hold promise, they pounded and blasted at its mountains. Because it is isolated, they holed up here. This theme of man in direct, inescapable relation to nature — of human ecology — is the overriding theme. Whether 17th-century Spaniard or 20th-century miner, the relation was much the same.

At this level environmental interpretation acts as a time machine. It helps people get out of their cultural and temporal skins so that they can experience the natural world as their ancestors (genetically, their ancestral selves) once did. Immersion in a non-insulated natural world is necessary if technological man is to understand himself as natural man. Unless pain is felt, it is abstraction. Unless a human being feels the boundaries of nature, he forgets that they are there.

Nobody at this level of environmental interpretation is talking about environmental reform as such; there is no need to. Bringing men back to direct confrontation with nature is to demonstrate that there is no escape from nature. Granted general understanding of this basic fact, environmental conservation will cease being a matter of voluntary good deeds and be instead an involuntary natural act, like breathing.

A step beyond the direct and personal confrontation with nature is the anthropological level of environmental encounter. The Pueblo Indians of the Southwest, using very simple tools, lived self-sufficiently for hundreds of years in places where technological man would die, lacking imports of water, food, and fuel. We tend to view technological man as powerful, pretechnological man as weak. But what is the truth? The Pueblo Indian was a consummate scrounger. In country that looks moon-barren to us he could find (or, with fine technology, produce) all he needed of water, food, and material. The Indian didn't need very much to get by; we need a lot to get by. In this light who is more vulnerable: an Indian who needs little and knows how to get it, or a technological man who needs much and is running out? To put it another way, if the technostructure fails which would you rather have: a burro or a Boeing 747?

Story-line interpretation in prehistoric areas has unlimited scope for treatment of such paradoxes. They may highlight modern man's dilemma (success as supertech man means failure as biological man), or they may demonstrate the value systems and operating techniques of other men who were more at home with the earth than we are.

The objective of this blended natural/historical dimension interpretation is simple: It squelches the great science-will-save-us-in-the-end myth. It talks straight to the fiction of unlimited power. It puts teeth back into natural laws that will prevail. It shows that technological man doesn't have to go on violating his mother, the earth; that he can instead learn from people of other cultures and times how to use technology sparingly, how to live off the interest of the earth instead of mining its capital, how to demand from the earth only what he needs, how to substitute for gross, nest-fouling materialism a life style that measures quality by inner satisfactions.

The historical dimension, once enlisted in the service of environmental interpretation, turns into a Pandora's Box (if one is afraid) or a treasure trove of opportunities (if one is secure).

Most public or quasi-public historical interpretation hews to the Fourth of July level of rhetorical generality, or, alternately, burrows deep in antiquarian specialization. The result is heroic, glorified political history; buttons-and-bows social history. Reinforcing these banal, non-controversial expressions is a whole set of anachronistic premises, objectives, and constraints: First, that the men and events of the past are uniformly honorable, even if sometimes mistaken. Second, that the white, northern European — infused with Godliness and virtue — is the only moving force of U.S. history. Third, that the tragic sense of history is a no-no because it would violate the Manifest Destiny-Progress-Optimism-Chosen of God syndrome that justifies all phases of U.S. history. Fourth, that history is a kind of nationalistic myth machine that should neither jeopardize the making of patriots nor sully the wistful nostalgia of white, middle-class citizens.

Perpetuation of this kind of historical interpretation is a disservice to the public. This is a time when value systems are in flux. People are insecure. They need to know just how tough and confused and oft-times tragic the past really was. Otherwise the tough and confused and oft-times tragic present may seem too unfair a blow. The men who signed the Declaration weren't acting out some predestined morality play, God the prompter with string ensemble accompaniment; they were traitors sweating out the hangman's noose, plotting to get rid of the Royalists who would betray them.

Until U.S. history is interpreted in a way that shows how temporal and selective our national good fortune has been, how based on geographic and environmental luck (as opposed to superior virtue), we will continue to be millinarians and missionaries pursuing disastrous policies at home and abroad — but comforted by the illusion that divine intervention will save us if things go too far wrong. Robert Heilbroner's *The Future as History*[5] speaks profoundly to this point.

Official history has crammed our minds and textbooks with myths (textbook committees are myth keepers) that seem to exempt us from the historical imperatives that constrain other nations. This form of historical hubris is little different from the natural hubris that seems to exempt us from environmental imperatives. Both kinds of arrogance are refusals to recognize the limits of power. In combination the two kinds of arrogance — superiority over other people, superiority over nature — make dubious the certainty of a future.

Confidence based on historical myth is today challenged by doubt based on historical fact. Materialism based on false notions of environmental infinitude is challenged by metaphysics based on the truth of environmental finiteness. The loud, rich extrovert — product of the myths — becomes progressively more quiet, more concerned with things of the spirit.

The historical dimension, as a field for environmental interpretation, must sooner or later reflect the evolution and the needs of the American people, for they are challenged as never before. And if there are,

---

[5]   Harper and Row, New York, 1960.

indeed, lessons to be learned, perspectives to be gained from history, now is the time.

¶ Each generation rewrites history so that it makes sense in an evolving value system. This does not mean that historians are simply expedient; nor does it imply perversion of historical fact. It does mean that the same facts mean different things in different eras, and that selection of facts out of the past is influenced by current concerns.

A simple example: Fifty years ago the exploits of Thomas A. Edison were viewed through the value-system lens of that time. America had just won a war; it had proved to the world that it was a growing, powerful nation. The time had come to return from abroad and realize the continental dream of development and exploitation. The wonders of radio and rural electrification were opening whole new worlds to people until then almost as isolated and sundown-bound as Asian peasants. Electricity powered these accomplishments. Electricity was, in the context of the times, an unalloyed blessing. The historian of that time — reflecting the prevailing values, himself an enthusiastic participant in the electrically powered social and economic revolution — could do no less than enshrine Edison and praise the results of his work with hosannahs.

A historian today, understanding the values of that time, would not necessarily debunk the earlier interpretation. But he would very legitimately add some sobering facts to the narrative — reflecting today's environmental concerns. Electricity an unalloyed blessing? Hardly. Rampant technology, growth, and industrialization, synonyms for all that's good? Not quite. The inventor, scientist, technician, engineer a demigod? — or as we have learned over and over again in the last 50 years, the embodiment of the cutting and often irresponsible edge of infinite human demand in a finite world?

Out of this new interpretation and the questions it raises come the perspectives that fit our era of environmental crisis. Edison and his inventions become precursors of today's scientific-technological dynamo — which, as correctly foreseen by Edison's contemporary, Henry Adams, drives us toward environmental disaster and spiritual dissolution. The historian has not discredited Edison, but he has forced a critical look at the world that Edison's inventions — proliferated beyond natural limits — have wrought. And if the historian has done his job as environmental interpreter, he has provoked people to wonder about the future being hatched for them by today's scientists and technologists.

The historian who finds himself interpreting nuclear energy sites dives immediately into the environmental soup. The scientists who opened the atomic age knew immediately that they had unleashed a Frankenstein. Today, nuclear energy for war pushes the world ever closer to instant holocaust. Nuclear energy for peace is heralded as the wave of the future — just as electricity was — even though many scientists fear its operational dangers and the incredible potency and longevity of its waste poisons.

Interpretation of Trinity Site, where the first atomic bomb was exploded in July 1945, could be inane, dealing with the big bang as though it were a super Fourth of July firework. Interpretation might go beyond that, treating the bomb as the product of a qualitatively new mobilization of science and technology — landmark in the history of science, prototype of today's great research and development complexes. But that, too, would be superficial.

Any interpretive program at Trinity Site that failed to provoke deep pondering over the moral and pragmatic issues created by the atomic bomb would be a travesty. The first atomic bomb — symbol of the atomic age in all its manifestations — poses every possible question about the survival of man. No aspect of the physical environment, the social environment, nor the individual life remains untouched by nuclear energy in the hands of man. Here is the end product of the apple in Eden. Here is man as Prometheus — having stolen the fire of the Gods, how will he use it? The total environment is at stake.

¶ It is almost a cliché for the social scientist to put the monkey of responsibility on the pure scientist's back. Physicists and bio-chemists who tinker with the hinges of the universe are natural fall guys — along with the engineers who do the dirty work. The social scientist asks, "Why did you not foresee the potential for evil in this formula, that machine?"

On the other hand, the social scientist — sensitive because his "science" is less than pure — takes pride in his objectivity. He digs up facts and statistics, but avoids value judgments as to their meaning. Thus, ironically, does the social scientist choose the role of mere technician. But this is delusion. "One's values and social objectives inevitably pervade the most abstruse of scholarly research. The good [social scientist] identifies, states, and pursues the ethical goals that he treasures most highly. Value-free social science is both impossible and abominable."[6]

This circumlocution brings us to another phase of historical interpretation. Some old-school historians tend to view their trade as a genteel art, whose subject matter is appropriate only for gilt-edged volumes, panelled club rooms, and gatherings of venerable mem-

---

6 Robert Lekachman, reviewing Gunnar Myrdal's *The Challenge of World Poverty,* in *Saturday Review,* Oct. 3, 1970, p. 35.

bers of venerable historical societies. History in these circles avoids unpleasantries, or euphemizes them so that they are palatable in an atmosphere where taste comes first.

For good reason Colonial Williamsburg, the splendid restoration of Virginia's 18th-century capital, merits its reputation as the apotheosis of historic site development and operation in this country. Painstaking research assures authenticity of physical environment and living exhibits. A harmonious blend of scholarship, technical virtuosity, and dramatic skill informs interpretive programs that make the 18th century come alive. The upshot is a setting conducive to the image of the young Jefferson strolling with his William and Mary classmates, absorbed in learned discourse and absorbing from the carefully designed gardens and neo-classical architecture the concepts of balance and restraint that would dignify his political philosophy. This evocation of atmospherics, of the intangible moods and modes of an era, marks the highest expression of the interpretive art. Yet, in major respects Colonial Williamsburg, and many similar historical restorations, obscure the history of yesterday and fail the society of today.

Dr. W.A.R. Goodwin inspired John D. Rockefeller, Jr., to restore Williamsburg. The two men had faith that ". . . the authentic environment of an important place in a formative century of American history brought back to life could furnish present-day visitors with historical perspective and with inspiration to become better citizens."[7] A few months before the 1926 decision to

---

[7] Edward P. Alexander, *The Interpretation Philosophy of Colonial Williamsburg,* Colonial Williamsburg, Inc., Williamsburg, Va., mimeographed, 1964, p. 1.

restore, Dr. Goodwin wrote:

> If you have ever walked around Williamsburg late on a moonlight night ... and felt the presence and companionship of the people who used to live here ... and remembered the things that they did and the things that they stood for ... and [recalled what] they said in the House of Burgesses and at the old College — you would then know what an interesting place Williamsburg is.[8]

And in 1937 Mr. Rockefeller stated his view of the value of the restoration:

> As the work has progressed, I have come to feel that perhaps an even greater value is the lesson that it teaches of the patriotism, high purpose, and unselfish devotion of our forefathers to the common good.[9]

Built into these statements of inspiration and aspiration is a limiting frame that today still circumscribes the operation of Colonial Williamsburg, Inc. They set the tone for the particular octave of history that Williamsburg recreates. They also define the visitor.

Who are the present-day visitors, and who are their ghostly 18th-century companions, and what is the critical affinity between them? Finally, who is left out?

As documented by Williamsburg's own surveys, most visitors are well off and well educated. Given the facts of U.S. demography, that means that they are overwhelmingly middle or upper class whites.

The Founding Fathers, as that term is usually construed, were all white men.

Now, this does leave out quite a few people — historically and today. Half the people of historic Williamsburg were Negro slaves. Williamsburg and its plantation hinterland was the headquarters of Greek democracy in America. As in ancient Greece, Williamsburg was governed by an oligarchy of aristocrats

---

8 *Ibid.*, p. 2.

9 *Ibid.*

(supported by slaves) who indulged in politics, literature, art, and bucolic delights.

In this light, who is a forefather, and of what does his devotion to the common good consist? Was he black? Was his devotion signified by jolly good humor as his family was auctioned off to foreign parts at the Williamsburg slave market? Or was this black forefather's contribution an impassioned plea for liberty in the House of Burgesses? And whom did he want to be free of, King George or his owner?

If I were a black man today I would find very little invitation in the Colonial Williamsburg concept and interpretive program. Conceptually it treats blacks as non-persons (*Our* forefathers? *The* Founding Fathers?). The interpretive milieu glosses over and omits vast areas of history — like one-half of the human history of Williamsburg. As in so many other places, the black who comes to Williamsburg is a faceless person, because he is not acknowledged as having had forefathers; nor are they credited with making Williamsburg's Golden Age possible.

There are school programs, foreign visitor programs, and others that touch upon slavery in the context of plantation and industrial life. But the basic thrust of Williamsburg interpretation — as to both topic and visitor target — is as white as the driven snow. It cannot help but be that way in the limited cultural framework of Colonial Williamsburg, Inc.

Grasp the subtle meaning of it. This ethnocentric exclusiveness springs not from racist design. Rather, cultured men allowed it to happen as a kind of oversight, an inadvertence dictated by custom. After all, as the historian says, the slaves of Williamsburg *didn't* make history! Washington, Jefferson, Mason, Madison — *The* Founding Fathers — made history!

Then put yourself in the black man's position. He went to Williamsburg as a school child — before changing times got out of hand. He saw history through the white lenses handed to him at Williamsburg. He saw black men as affable "folks" in the background of what was important — quiet and dutiful, and watched over so that their imprudent ways wouldn't get them into trouble. Would you want your daughter . . . to be fed such a perversion of history?

¶ At this point, it is necessary to pause and digest. If this critique of Colonial Williamsburg, Inc., is at all valid, it begins with history itself: The founding concepts of Colonial Williamsburg, Inc., the institutional framework that gives form to those concepts, the interpretive programs that convey them to visitors, and the visitors themselves are all prisoners of history.

But there are two kinds of history: that which has been made already, and that which is being made now. Colonial Williamsburg, like the rest of us, is prisoner of both. It is bound in every explicit way by the past — which includes not only the 18th century, but also the view of the 18th century held 40 years ago by Messrs. Goodwin and Rockefeller. Less well recognized is the fact that Colonial Williamsburg is also caught in the main currents and forces of today's history-in-the-making. To the extent that it fails to evolve out of the older bonds, it becomes anachronistic in today's world, an antique to be stored in the attic rather than a vital force in an evolving society.

It is necessary, therefore, to place Colonial Williamsburg (the symbol of historic preservation everywhere) into today's context, to make it responsive to today's needs. The basic justification for an evolving sensitivity to current concerns is to be found in the above-quoted words of Dr. Goodwin and Mr. Rockefeller. When all that they said is distilled, they wanted Colonial Williamsburg to *function* in the world of the present (1970's as well as 1930's) to the ends of good citizenship and the common good.

Such ends simply must apply across the pluralistic board of America today. That means that the average black citizen — descendent of slaves — must find personal dignity at Williamsburg, through knowledge of the contributions of his ancestors; he must also find identification with the very Founding Fathers who owned his ancestors, because the highest ideals of these men forever trapped Americans in the pursuit of equality.

Such are the paradoxes and tensions that historical interpretation everywhere must tackle. To do so, interpreters must get rid of the variously tinted glasses that make history one thing for one group, and another thing for another group. The past, just as the present, must be accepted for what it thought and what it was — that means the whole truth, the good and the bad, the thick and the thin, the black and the white.

It must be acknowledged that Colonial Williamsburg does reflect current concerns by hosting youth forums and conducting other special interpretive efforts. But such special (a black reads *token*) efforts fail to do the job. They bespeak precisely the attitude that Black America so deeply resents: "Well, we can only do so much; it just wouldn't be practical to start over." But of course that's what it will take.

Colonial Williamsburg can respond to the special needs of black citizens, which ramify throughout our national life, making them a reflection of urgent national need. Through its interpretive programs it can say in myriad ways, "We see you! We hear you! We recognize you and your forefathers as persons! You have been in the crucible of Williamsburg's history from the beginning!" In this way, as it has been a leader in so many other respects, Colonial Williamsburg could now make historical interpretation a living force for social cohesion — in a country that cries for it.*

Story-line interpretation has been the interpreter's home ground for so long that it's hard to break away. To wrap it up, I want to list some germinal story-line ideas and applications, as a series of *Item reports*, then end by discussing a strategy for interpretive planning.

Item: *Environmental interpretation, story-line and otherwise, must reach many audiences. Each person, in fact, is a different "audience" because each one brings to the interpretive experience his own bundle of ideas about the environment and what it means to him.* Some of the cue cards that visitors might flash at an interpreter are discussed by Clarence J. Glacken in an essay "The Man-Nature Theme,"[10] which is outlined below:

Western man has had a number of big ideas about the world around him and his place in it. Three of the most important are *Teleology*, *Web of Life*, and *Ecosystem*, in that historical order.

Teleology has given us a two-way view of nature. First, the earth and its contents were made for man to *use*. This view, with many historical accretions, has led to the notion that anything goes; the system will right itself; God (or Science) will intervene in man's behalf. The second view, stemming from the same generic source, is exemplified by Saint Francis of Assisi — love of and companionship with God's creatures—an attitude of sharing the earth with other living things.

The *Web of Life* idea came into vogue as a corollary to Darwinism. It stressed the relationships between living things and their physical surroundings. It stemmed from the concept of evolution of species.

---

*Editor's Note: Ralph W. Ellison, author and lecturer, became the first black appointed to the Colonial Williamsburg, Inc., Board of Trustees in March, 1971.

10 Clarence J. Glacken, "Reflections On The Man-Nature Theme As A Subject For Study," in *Future Environments of North America*, F. Fraser Darling and John P. Milton, eds., Natural History Press, Garden City, N.Y., 1966, pp. 355-371.

Modern *Ecosystem* science has expanded upon the Web of Life, defining ever-more complex relationships between communities, ever-larger ecosystems, until the world and all its animate and inanimate elements are seen in inextricable, interdependent relationship.

From these germinal ideas have come many attitudes. Here are some of them:

1. *Anthropocentrism*

   Use nature.

   Be humble before the creation.

   Pathetic fallacy ("the sky wept"; "the sea raged").

2. *Communion with Nature*

   The belief that in the solitudes of nature are to be found authentic manifestations of the life-giving forces; that knowledge, emotional reinforcement, and inspiration . . . come from that special kind of solitude found in the presence of nature.

   Corollary: Cities are bad; the "good" environment is that one farthest from man, i.e., wilderness.

3. *The Beauty, Variety, and Complexity of Nature*

   God's bounty idea.

   Scientific and esthetic concern for threatened species.

The modern ecologist's belief that complexity is the requisite of environmental stability.

4. *Posterity Argument*

Save something for the kids.

Stewardship.

Avoid irreversible trends.

5. *Tourism*

The Grand Tour.

Wealth, mobility, art and photography.

Appreciation of scenery as a constructive force in environmental conservation.

Tourism and trampling.

Cosmopolitan tourism as a counterforce against utilitarian gobbling up of beauty spots because of the press of population and poverty.

6. *Protection of Varieties of Environments for Scientific Study and Research*

Man will lose irreplaceable varieties of life; the genetic pool reduced (genetic strains that may give man a chance to reconstruct degraded environments).

Variety and complexity of world ecosystem.

109

Ecumenism of science, a force for environmental conservation that transcends nations, religions.

¶ If environmental interpretation is primarily aimed at attitudinal change, modification, or reinforcement, it's good to know some of the attitudes people start with. Each of these attitudes (and others not mentioned, e.g., the urbanite's fear of or indifference to "nature") is a different cue card for the interpreter.

Probably the Posterity Argument is the strongest, because it is easily understood and emotionally loaded. But what of the attitudes we have neglected, or held in disdain (Tourism, for example)? Each attitude is in effect a built-in response mechanism, a motivator to action. Each person has one or more of these attitudes. To get to our visitors we must be able to spot their idea-attitude affinities and adapt our interpretive approaches to them.

Item: *To get a feel for the ways and means to provoke visitor participation in the interpretive process (instead of passively soaking up facts) check out the new "inquiry method" textbooks now invading the schools.* An exemplary social studies text (middle grades) with much substance and technique directly transferable to interpretive contexts, is Martin W. Sandler, *et al.*, *The People Make a Nation.*[11] A quote from the teacher's edition shows the similarity between the inquiry method in education and the provocational method in interpretation:

---

[11] From the Teachers' Edition of *The People Make a Nation* by Martin W. Sandler, Edwin C. Rozwenc, and Edward C. Martin. ©Copyright 1971 by Allyn and Bacon, Inc. Reprinted by permission of Allyn and Bacon, Inc.

The People Make a Nation provides materials for the student which will help him to discover and understand the people and events that contributed to the making of this nation. This book provides many kinds of evidence to enable students to come to meaningful conclusions about the shaping and reshaping of institutions that form the basic structure of American society. . . .

. . . The emphasis of the "new social studies" is inquiry learning. Inquiry must begin with questions. Each of the eight Units in this book presents a basic question. These Unit questions have present-day as well as historical relevance. Indeed, historians and social scientists continue to seek answers to them. The student searches for answers to the Unit question in firsthand accounts by people who took part in the making of this nation and in secondary accounts by historians and other literary figures. Usually these accounts reflect contrasting opinions and interpretations. For example, the views of a slave are presented along side those of a slave owner. The opinions of those who saw the coming of the machine as a beneficial development in man's history are contrasted with the opinions of those who saw the machine as an eventual threat to man. Readings have been chosen for student interest as well as for historical importance. . . .

The Unit questions from this text hint at the depth of social studies probing made possible by the inquiry method:

    I. FOUNDERS AND FOREFATHERS
       Who were the people who made America?

   II. GOVERNMENT BY THE PEOPLE
       Can it be made to work?

  III. MODERN POLITICS IN AMERICA
       How did it come about?

  IV. SLAVERY AND SEGREGATION
       Did the Civil War change America?

Item: *Whenever possible, work into story-line interpretation the relationship between the state of health of the biosphere and the state of health of individual people.* There is a temptation to hold public health topics for clearinghouse/forum interpretation. To do so misses great interpretive opportunities and deprives great numbers of casual visitors (who don't stick around for deep probing) of this key insight: Environmental reform goes beyond esthetics; it strikes at the fundamental conditions for healthy human life.

In interpreting a number of prehistoric Pueblo sites, for example, public health factors that forced the ancient people to abandon their homes are different only in time, place, and scale from public health problems faced by urban America today: exhausted agricultural lands producing non-nutritious foods; inadequate or spoiled water; disease from too many people crowding into limited space, compounded by the accumulation of solid wastes.

Interpretation of industrial and agricultural sites opens the door on such public health problems as noise, air, water, and pesticide pollution, black-lung disease, and similar industrial afflictions.

Water recreation sites, especially reservoirs for domestic and industrial water supplies, should conduct hard-line environmental interpretation on all fronts to show how hard it is to maintain water quality. At the natural history level, for example, a blend of story-line and resource management interpretation can show eutrophication in action (a man-accelerated natural phenomenon), and then show how environmental managers are trying to cut the inflow of the sewage and industrial wastes that produce the algae blooms.

All natural history interpretation can be translated into human public health terms by simple analogy. If a naturalist is describing parasitism he can show how some parasites restrain themselves so as not to kill their hosts, how others greedily drain their hosts dry and die with them. Potential analogies with human behavior are almost infinite in this single example. The pedant can get all hung up on the degrees of parasitism, but then he misses a great interpretive vehicle: Generally, predators consume their capital but parasites live off the interest. Even more subtle: Some parasites and hosts evolved from that relationship into one that is symbiotic. How many things does this say to man and his relationship to the rest of the biosphere?

The healthy biome, with its system of checks and balances based on variety and complexity, contrasts all too obviously with biomes altered by man. Having simplified them, thus destroying the natural checks and balances, man then must intervene with poisons, which come back in food, water, and air to poison the poisoner.

One quick foray into military history hints at the many ways it can illustrate current environmental and public health problems: What was the rationale for Sherman's March through Georgia during the Civil War? Simply, this campaign and others like it made environments occupied by the enemy uninhabitable. The destroying armies cut forests, opened floodgates, burned crops, poisoned water. The victims of this total warfare fled the country, the weak died, disease swept the land. In modern warfare, man's expanded technology increases environmental destruction. Indeed, "War is not good for children and other living things."

Item: *The aspiring environmental interpreter who is stuck with old-line (non-environmental) interpretive facilities and programs can devise many updating options.* These options *don't* include waiting for the millenium when he gets money to redo everything, nor patching and fiddling and mongrelizing exhibits so that they lose their old integrity and aren't any good environmentally either. For examples, here are a few starters: Special rotating exhibits can be used as environmental conversation pieces, brightening up a museum hall, a visitor lobby, a reception room. Easily fabricated or purchased AV programs (slide shows, film strips, recordings of poems and music) can be substituted for old-line irrelevant ones. Surprise environmental messages (simple photo and caption exhibits) can be spotted at key points. A set of old exhibits that conveys a lot of good environmentalism, but isn't synthesized or explicit enough, *can* be synthesized and made explicit by an integrating slide program, an introductory orientation talk, or a short text handout. Look over your old-line interpretive facilities and determine how to insert light additive touches that turn them into effective environmental communications.

Item: *Sometimes story-line and resource-management interpretation can be combined in most interesting fashion.* An example: At a Western historic site commemorating the cattleman's era, the interpreter got local school children interested in restoring a plot of rangeland to its historic appearance. Native grasses had been replaced with weeds long before, because of overgrazing that had changed the character of the range. Therefore, the native grasses were an elusive factor, and recreating soil conditions that would support them wasn't easy. This set of questions led the students into historical research and work with botanists and soil scientists. When they got the answers, they ordered seed and sowed it and tended the plot of ground until it fitted the descriptions in historical documents. They topped off the project with a rodeo and barbecue.

These children are descendants of pioneer ranchers. Their parents are still ranchers, and many of the kids will be, too. In this project, history and biology came together for the students in a larger environmental mix, one of personal interest to them. They got to know their pioneer ancestors a little better. They learned about range management by being range managers. And, incidentally, they recreated an historical environment.

To conclude this section on story-line interpretation, we shift from particular approaches and applications to a higher level — *the strategy of interpretive planning.* Almost any enterprise can be broken down into the Why, the What, and the How. In story-line interpretation these three conceptual levels can be phrased as the Objective, the Theme, and the Medium. In setting up an interpretive program, the first thing to do is figure out the objective. Why are you exposing the visitor to this encounter with history, nature, or whatever?

Quoted below is a broad-scope interpretive objective meant to shape and give coherence to interpretive programs of the National Wildlife Refuge System:[12]

To accomplish the objectives of the interpretive program in

---

[12] H. Jesse Grove, "The Preface," in *Interpretation in the National Wildlife Refuge System,* Bureau of Sport Fisheries and Wildlife, U.S. Dept. of the Interior, Wash., D.C., mimeographed, 1969.

the National Wildlife Refuge System, we must re-mold the existing image of a National Wildlife Refuge in the eyes of the *broad* spectrum of the American citizenry. This refining of the refuge image must highlight the point that these areas are indeed "communities of life," and miniatures or models of the total ecosystem or environmental process in which the visitor and his own community, urban or rural, is a part. Interpretation must bridge the gap between the artificial world of the visitor and the natural world of the refuge. In many existing interpretive programs, the visitor too often carries away with him disjointed pieces of natural history information — much as he may collect a sea shell from a beach and know only that it is a shell — an end product, and know nothing of the reasons for its being.

This objective provides a flexible framework that can fit around any wildlife refuge. The refuge and its regional setting supply themes for the interpretive program. Is it a coastal flyway refuge catering to migratory birds? If so, the standard interpretive themes — such as kinds of birds, their feeding habits, their migration routes — become launch pads for hard-line environmental themes: What is happening to estuaries because of petrochemical plants, oil spills, dredging, and sewage dumping? What does this mean to the biological health of the estuary? What happens to the migratory birds when they have no place left to feed and rest? What about people who come to see the birds? And how about folks who like to eat shellfish, which are dying from estuarine poisoning? What about the myth that says: When the land gets too fouled up we can get our food from the ocean? "By the way, have you read *The Fragile Ocean* by Wesley Marx? ... Well, just by coincidence I've got a copy for sale back in the office ...."

This book does not discuss the details of presentation technique, types of AV hardware, exhibit fabrication and the like. The technical literature treats these matters, and technicians are the ones who can help set up a facility or program. But one hint on media and techniques will be useful: Before making final decision on the means of environmental communication, bring your visitors into the act. Ask them what they would like, what would aid their understanding. This simple procedure breaks the unhealthy monopoly of the experts — who often disregard the visitor. It's hard to remember sometimes that environmental communications and reform have a warm human objective: healthy, happy people. If this objective is not worked into the process, it won't be part of the product.

Success in the planning of story-line environmental interpretation depends, first and foremost, on the successful definition of objective. Next in sequence and importance comes the derivation of themes from the resource itself. Finally comes the technical phase of selecting, fabricating, and installing media. This order of significance — from objective to themes to media — may help interpreters get off the hook of fooling with technical innovation for its own sake because they haven't figured out a message worth delivering.

¶ *Resource management interpretation is implicit in every management act.* For convenience we can classify those acts in the way that they eventually affect natural and man-made physical resources: First, those acts that degrade environments; second, those acts that restore degraded environments; third, those acts that produce symbiotic man/environment relationships.

Overlaps between these categories emerge as we begin to work with them. For example, interpretation of environmental mismanagement includes not only recital of mistakes (a structure built on unstable geologic foundations) but also lessons learned (don't build on bentonite, i.e., understand the geology of proposed building sites before deciding to build on them), and corrective action contemplated, underway, or accomplished (removal of building to favorable site, where management objectives conform to environmental imperatives).

From another viewpoint, the three-fold classification describes the *stages* of the environmental management process: from mismanagement, to rectification, to man/environment symbiosis. This leads to the conclusion that environmental mismanagement is a proper, indeed essential, subject for environmental interpretation.

Concrete, on-site examples of the mistake-rectification-symbiosis process are the best handles for resource management interpretation. With them, the interpreter can help the visitor get a bite-sized perspective on world-wide man/environment problems. Lacking such tangible, demonstrable examples, ecology and environmental management remain abstractions. And the visitor, confused by it all, too easily repeats the comforting formula: "Well, I guess the experts will have to tackle those problems."

This response zaps the principal objective of environmental interpretation: to encourage public participation in environmental management/reform action. Such participation requires that the public have faith in itself — faith among concerned citizens that they, too, can use the principles of environmental management to rectify the botched environments where they live.

Resource management interpretation, using concrete example and application, develops two basic concepts: bio-politics and bio-economics. These concepts stand in opposition to business-as-usual politics and economics, which usually sacrifice the environment to expediency.

The dialogue of expediency has a familiar ring: Is it a question of park or recreation area boundaries? Then make them small so as not to arouse land-owners and legislators; don't worry about watersheds and other natural limits. Where to route the highway? Through the park to avoid high costs and condemnation proceedings elsewhere. How to plan the area? To meet the demands of the loudest, most politically potent segment of the public, whatever the effects on the environment (usually meaning more campgrounds, more roads, more concessions). Development program versus inadequate funding? Make it look good on the cheap; maintenance can pick up the pieces later. Where to align the road? On the budget contours. Ecological research before building? Hell no, don't have the time or the talent; eyeball the site, then let 'er rip. Stop the mistake or the destructive program? No, finish the project; satisfy the clientele public.

Whether dealing with in-house, in-boundary environmental management problems, or with regional plans and developments, the resource manager constantly confronts the business-as-usual attitudes and decisions just parodied. Interpretation of this constant struggle deals with results: Did business-as-usual politics/economics or bio-politics/economics win? And why? What were the forces, internal and external, that forced the management decisions that produced the results we see?

The objective of this kind of interpretation is to demonstrate to the public (whether casual visitors or citizen participants working with the manager to preserve the resource and its regional context) the *environmental consequences* of the opposing kinds of politics and economics.

This is less a finger-pointing exercise, based on the black hat-white hat dichotomy, than it is a dispassionate look at the results of modern environmentalism versus cultural lag. Unless the public is allowed to know *why* environmental successes or failures occur, all manner of pieties about environmental ethics go down the drain.

This interpretive approach strikes deep at management behavior. To the extent that a manager's environmental successes and failures are shared with the public, which is the fall guy when we mismanage public property, managers are forced to fight the good environmental fight. Failure to do so invites public contempt . . . and unfavorable ramifications up the organizational line, where images rise or fall. The old days of management prerogative and secrecy are over anyway, so we might as well enlist public concern as a self-enforcing mechanism to keep us on the environmental straight and narrow . . . and to give us clout when we decide to fight environmental mismanagement, from whatever source.

Using the parent concepts of bio-politics and bio-economics, the interpreter, whether dealing with a very specific localized problem (like a poorly constructed trail) or a massive, regional insult (like the power-plant system) can develop many handles for visitor understanding. For example, the trail, poorly laid out and cheaply built, produces many dis-economies, expressed as esthetic and environmental degradation and the costs of chronic maintenance. The dis-economies of the power plants, expressed as polluting, poisonous by-products, lead to an extension of the dis-economy idea: It is quite obvious that society is no longer in the mood to allow a business or industry to *externalize* its dis-economies, i.e., make them somebody else's headache (the guy downstream or downwind). Rather, by legislation and regulation, we (society) must extend the producer's responsibility so that his dis-economy is internalized (becomes his own headache or profit).

Through environmental interpretation, we must share in the necessary task of giving people this new perspective of bio-economics and bio-politics. The basic message is that the economics and politics of expediency produce environmental debits, which all of us, one day, will have to pay for. Thus, in this new perspective, what appears economical and expedient today may be just the opposite tomorrow.

Here we slide into environmental cost accounting, which attaches value to things difficult to quantify. How much *does* a mature tree in a park cost — in dollars and cents? What is the value of a park in terms of social health — in dollars and cents? Above all, what is the *replacement cost* of such things?

Replacement costs should be figured into the contracts that represent economic decisions and into the taxes that represent political decisions. Then the easy way out (let's sacrifice the park, the wildlife refuge, the neighborhood, the coastline, Lake Erie) will be seen as the hard way. Because it will be realized that someday the mistakes must be undone. It was easy to ruin Lake Erie, but it will cost billions to restore it; and it must be done to save the Great Lakes region.

Enlightened resource management depends on getting true readings (understanding ecological determinants) from the biosphere. *How* we get true readings, and how we apply them, form the basis of resource management interpretation. Ian McHarg, in a summary of six elements of ecological determinism, outlines this approach to stewardship.[13] Using these elements as a kind of checklist he shows how natural processes dictate human adaptations to the environment, or, if ignored, invite disaster. For example, igloos in the Arctic and stilt houses in marshes are ecologically determined. By contrast, the wildly non-ecological development of the New Jersey barrier islands (breaching seaward dunes with roads, destruction of stabilizing plant cover, concrete slab construction) led to the hurricane wipe-out of 1962.

---

[13] Ian L. McHarg, "Ecological Determinism," in *Future Environments of North America,* pp. 526-538.

Here are McHarg's six elements:

1. *Ecosystem Inventory.* Produces the knowledge that is the basis for planning and development related to natural processes.

2. *Description of Natural Processes.* Supplements static inventories and maps with process data (e.g., ecosystem succession).

3. *Identification of Limiting Factors.* Critical factors necessary to perpetuation of the ecosystem (e.g., fresh-brackish balance in estuarine waters).

4. *Attribution of Value.* The replacement cost concept (dollars-and-cents quantification as a buttress to esthetic or ecologic values).

5. *Determination of Prohibitions and Permissiveness to Change.* Identification of the constraints inherent to natural processes which should affect the location and nature of development.

6. *Indicators of Stability or Instability.* Those environmental signals that warn of pathology or confirm health, whether of natural or man-made environments (entropy in a pond ecosystem; rats in a ghetto).

The resource manager can use these elements as a checklist when he converts the results of area or regional management into interpretive programs. If he is interpreting a success, he can check off adherence to the six elements. If he is interpreting failure, he can identify the elements overlooked in the management process, and specify the consequences. Such interpretation cannot avoid the human ecology of environmental management: Successful managers and management systems abide by ecological determinants; unsuccessful ones don't.

The essential setting for resource management interpretation is the demonstration site itself. If a poorly built road is making a mountain collapse, then go to that place to interpret the environmental management failure. On-site the interpreter can point out the slumping strata, the emergency stabilization measures, the esthetic mess. Here he can tell why it all happened. The visitor, face to face with disaster, begins to understand the importance of environmental management. In this setting, because of his own involvement, he can be induced to volunteer opinions and options, which opens the door to critical discussion. Who isn't a sidewalk supervisor, if given a chance?

Similarly, if rehabilitation restores a degraded environment, get people out there to see the problem and the progress. An overused campground, put to pasture and reseeded, can be an exciting story of plant succession, a demonstration of nature's healing powers, if given a chance. A "scoreboard" in the form of record photos can demonstrate the site's rate of recovery. Get the botanists and soil scientists and engineers and maintenancemen to join the interpretive effort. They can tell about bad starts and lessons learned. In so telling they say much about the complexity of natural processes, and the patience required of men who would understand them, in order to work with them.

Where men have succeeded in working with environmental determinants, use the site to demonstrate the principles of symbiosis: structures that fit terrain and climate, and blend with underlying landscape realities; sound waste disposal practices; innovations that conserve fuel and water. In this way the physical plant of the park or recreation area becomes an environmental demonstration site — a window on the world that the visitor knows back home, where the same environmental challenges abound.

The environmental manager shows that he is *doing* the things, in his small plot, that all men must eventually do everywhere. To coin a thought, one demonstration of environmental management in action is worth 10,000 statements about what should be done.

Resource management interpretation, used to physically demonstrate the harmonies and disharmonies of man/environment relationships, packs much persuasive power. It counsels hope, because it shows that some men have taken the trouble to understand natural processes, and have reformed themselves — as individuals and as organizations — to work within those processes.

Ideally, this kind of interpretation contributes in at least three ways to the health and perpetuation of the park or recreation resource itself: First, it prods the manager to be a good environmental manager, *because* he wants to have something good to show. Second, by inviting the visitor into the family — making him privy to the inner councils of environmental management — he, too, learns to respect the area's environmental limits, and conforms to them. Ultimately, protection of quality environments depends on Everyman being his own environmentalist. Third, it leads especially interested segments of the public to participate as co-managers of the area; these are the people in universities and conservation groups who become the area's defenders against the pressures of degradation.

From the area base, established by story-line and resource management interpretation, the momentum and scope of environmental communiations grow — extending beyond the area into the society at large. At this point environmental interpretation shifts gears. The area becomes a platform, a resource that helps an aroused public translate its concerns into action.

The rest of this chapter treats the clearinghouse/ forum activities that lead to community action.

¶ Concerned people keep looking for an action focus. They sense the environmental problems surrounding them, pervading their society and community. Where can they grab off a piece of this big ball of wax? How can they extricate one of the worms from this tangled can?

Clearinghouse/forum interpretive functions set the stage for people to answer these questions. Viewed as sequence, the clearinghouse helps people identify the pieces and parts of the environmental puzzle, the forum brings people together to devise solutions and initiate action.

Both clearinghouse and forum appeal to two distinct types of citizen participants: those who are passing through, and those resident in the zone of influence of the park or recreation area.

For the "passing through" participant, the clearinghouse offers these interpretive media:

—*Special exhibits and programs describing environmental management problems of the area and its surrounding context.*

The object here is to illustrate the tangled skein that produces environmental problems, and the modes and stages that environmental managers employ to solve them. The man/man and man/environment relationships thus illustrated provide case studies and analogs that the visitor can apply to his own community.

For example, a water recreation area may receive sewage inflow from surrounding communities. Fish are dying, the lake is choking on algae. The resource and the communities both suffer, which creates a larger community of interest in environmental reform. The area manager initiates solution by working at the political and planning levels in his zone of influence. A regional watershed-management authority evolves to tie local jurisdictions together for coherent action. The authority develops a plan, which becomes the basis for a project grant from the Federal Water Quality Administration. The project results in a regional system that intercepts and treats sewage in a central plant, whence it is distributed as soil-enriching irrigation water to regional farms. The interpreter's job is to help visitors apply this case study to their own community problems.

—Environmental film and lecture-discussion programs.

—Environmental book and periodical racks, including hand-out folders, booklets, and mimeographed sheets with community-action suggestions.

The settings and atmospherics of such clearinghouse activities encourage, indeed provoke, visitor response, questions, and discussion with the interpreter. If your area has a visitor center with a lobby where people can sit down and rest, scatter a few pieces of environmental literature on a reading table. Consider them expendable; replace them *before* they get dog-eared and uninviting. The literature, along with eye-catching objects and exhibits, should be selected and designed to spur the visitor to ask a question or two of the interpreter — or make an assertion. Thus does an environmental discussion get born.

For residents of the resource area's zone of influence, the clearinghouse serves as a permanent community institution for the exchange of environmental information. Student and adult volunteers are invited to assist area personnel in this phase of clearinghouse activities. For example, they assemble data on existing or impending environmental problems in the region. Then they use area facilities for special programs describing these problems (e.g., plans for new roads, housing developments, and other land-use projects — which usually "happen" before the community-at-large has a chance to react at the political and planning levels).

Given a phone and a volunteer to help man it, the clearinghouse urges each citizen to be part of the community environmental early warning system. Often, observant citizens spot problems developing, but they don't know which government agency to call, or if they do, they get frustrated by the old "it's not in my department" game. The clearinghouse solves this communication problem by acting as a funnel. It receives complaints or warnings from citizens, then distributes them to the proper authorities. To put teeth in clearinghouse communications, the area manager initiates a regional coordinating council of environmental conservation groups. "Insurance" copies of all notifications to government authorities are sent to the coordinating council to assure a check on government response and action.

Areas that are centrally and conveniently located for community access and use emphasize on-site clearinghouse activities. Those geographically removed simply shift the scene of participation to off-site facilities — town hall, library, school, conservation group office, and the like.

Area sponsorship of and participation in the community clearinghouse function is not all altruism. Public relations benefits are obvious (and over the long haul will cancel out flak from violators of the community environment who are nailed by the clearinghouse). More important, the condition of the regional or zone-of-influence environment sets the tone for the area environment. In this light, investment of resources in clearinghouse activities is really a potent form of investment in environmental management.

Public forums are of two types: conference forums that bring together experts and notables to tackle major environmental trends and problems, and community forums that bring together residents of the resource area's zone of influence for community problem solving.

Conference forums are special meetings that occur once only or on a periodic basis. Professional groups might deal with broad-scope environmental topics on a state-wide or interstate basis — e.g., doctors on environmental health, teachers on environmental education, lawyers on environmental law. A specific example of a multidisciplinary gathering was the Summer 1970 International Symposium on Conditions for Human Survival at Grand Canyon National Park, Arizona, sponsored by the University of Utah Center for Environmental Biology.

The quality environments of park and recreation areas offer ideal settings for such meetings. People hammering out high environmental standards for society need inspirational surroundings as they labor — for the spirit of exploration and imagination must inform their efforts. As our quality environments stimulate reform action, they should also stimulate the esthetic and intellectual ferment that produces high aspiration.

Not every gathering or place can attract an international galaxy of notables as did the Grand Canyon symposium. But every extended community or region or state has academic, professional, and governmental resources that can be brought to bear on environmental problems.

The area manager seeking public support for coherent environmental management in his zone of influence could do no better thing than to initiate, sponsor, and host regional forums aimed at creating such support. Suppose the area context is being debauched by land developments that violate ecology and esthetics. A public forum on this problem would bring together a mix of the region's top people, along with the general public. The land rape that results from jurisdictional conflict and fragmentation would show the need for a regional land-use plan, supervised by a regional authority comprising all jurisdictions and interests. The public, edified by participation in the forum, then would have the basis of knowledge and the motivation to force political action to get such a plan and authority.

Extending the principle, regional forums could be held on environmental health, community and cross-cultural communications, economic development, and the standard pollution topics.

At this point the conference forum shades into the community forum — here visualized as a permanent, institutionalized mechanism for community environmental reform.

Throughout, this book has discussed standard environmental management/reform topics suitable for community forum discourse. Now let us concentrate on environmental interpretation as a positive force in the conservation, salvage, and improvement of *community life*. It is the urban or near-urban park or recreation resource that can have most effect on ameliorating the social disorganization of our cities. In this frame, management of the resource becomes a means to a social end, not an end in itself. That end is *life* in healthy diversity — the condition for *human life*.

From each resource base — whether individual unit or city or county system — a community to be served is identified. That community is defined as the *zone of effective interaction* between the resource base and the people whose life-way can be improved in some substantial degree by that resource.

Specifically, if the resource is to be truly relevant to the daily concerns of the community, that community must be defined *by its people* — in their terms of geography and aspiration. This means that park and recreation people must establish a new kind of rapport with their communities. Not the old one of knowing best, but a new one that presumes to know nothing about the community — one that seeks out the community's view of itself.

The park or recreation resource, having subordinated itself to the community's definition of itself and its needs, is effectively controlled by the community. Thus do the community's aspirations define the purpose and program of the resource.

Under this regime of community control — an expression of the community's life aspirations — environmental management and interpretation of the resource naturally follow. For a community's life aspirations define community environment.

The first tactic is to listen to your community clientele. At this stage environmental interpretation is the technique of helping people to tell themselves the truth about their community — by exploring these questions:

What is my community or neighborhood?

What do I really want my community or neighborhood to be like, to do for me?

What are the shibboleths, the intimidations that make my community less than it should be?

What are the pressure points for action to improve it?

How do I pool the friendly-to-life elements of my community to oppose the enemies of life?

This interpretive task — of assisting the community to see *what really is and what might be* — taps every discipline in park and recreation work:

> Managers of people can help show how a community is managed.

> A maintenance man can help show why a community is decaying physically.

> A historian can help show how time and events and personalities have shaped a community.

> A naturalist can as well classify and probe the relationships in human communities as he can the relationships in a forest or stream community.

> An anthropologist can shed light on modern subcultures as well as ancient ones.

> A planner or designer can help revive conditions for life.

The *actions* that follow definitions of need are manifold. It might be well to start with something bite-size, to get the feel of it — then keep rolling.

The fields for action? List the things wrong with our cities. Take water pollution. Not the waters of some far-away place. But the stuff that comes out of the tap; the river that rots the skin off the kids who swim in it anyway. Take hospitals. Do they reach beyond their walls to the sick people who need medical care, but aren't getting it? Do they conduct medical education programs as a form of preventive medicine? Take urban renewal. Is it killing the neighborhood? Does it displace poor people with no place to go? And on . . . and on . . . and on.

Every kind of park or recreation resource — using the broadest definition — should be in the thick of this community forum action. Every medium should be employed: from amateur theatre to speakers' bureaus to inter-agency cooperation that blends the efforts of playgrounds, parks, libraries, museums, community centers, schools, health clinics, social services, and churches. The community forum, linked with other citizen groups, should aim to fill the vacuum of political leadership that has sapped hope from city life.

This chapter began with a quotation about not pushing people up against the wall. Yet, I have been pretty blunt in my own mode of communication. My excuse is that this is an in-the-family book. We can afford to talk straight with one another on tactics because at the deep strategic level we are committed to the same objective: through our resources we try to help people experience the good life.

But environmental interpretation reaches beyond the family, to people not bound together by a common professional ethic. And environmental interpretation, as I have advocated it, will rub hard on many people. So I want to conclude this chapter by expanding on that notion about not pushing people up against the wall. What follows might be called an advocate's guide to communication: [14]

People attempting to lead public opinion must respect it as a fact of life, but without being intimidated or throwing in the towel.

Respect for and comprehension of the other man's views is the essential opening for the communication of persuasion.

A person is most likely to modify particular views if they are challenged in a way that does not assault his general values.

[14] Adapted from *Vietnam and the Silent Majority: A Dove's Guide,* by Milton J. Rosenberg, Sidney Verba and Philip E. Converse, Harper and Row, New York, 1970.

People who differ on particulars can still reach one another through the common links that bind them in "community."

People cannot communicate if, because of their views, they are made to feel alone.

People who agree on the need for environmental reform may disagree on many other issues.

Acknowledge the elements of truth in the views of those who disagree with you.

Listen.

interlude V

education
for survival

In a free society it is always the citizen
who must bear the ultimate responsibility
for the choices that are made and the actions
that are taken. In all our history we have
found no better way than through the process
of education for equipping citizens — you and
me and our children — with the knowledge and
understanding needed to make these choices
and to take these actions.

James E. Allen, Jr.
Former U.S. Commissioner
of Education

The enthusiasm, the idealism, and the untrammeled views of youth lend hope to the notion that mankind can learn to live in this world.

Today it is the "practical" man — caught in the net of custom and cultural lag — who perpetuates the systems of death. Locked in by the premises and assumptions of bygone times, anthropocentric and tribal in his outlook, he fails to leap the chasm from yesterday to today. This failure produces the ultimate impracticality: the refusal to be confused by the facts.

Today's youth starts from today's side of the chasm. Education informed by today's facts, education that puts the archaic facts of yesterday in their proper historical perspective, can keep youth on this side of the chasm.

Some scientists say we have a decade to tool up for fundamental environmental reform — a decade of lead time to devise the political and technological mechanisms that can reverse environmental destruction. During this decade, society's institutions take on a double task: at the operational level they *ameliorate* environmental crisis; at the research and development level they renew themselves for the fundamental work of *ending* environmental crisis.

In the broadest sense of the term, environmental education is society's principal instrument for accomplishing this double task. It must help adults cross the chasm and equip them for both operational and developmental tasks. Simultaneously, while adults hold the line and renew institutions, environmental education must equip youth, through experience and practice, to take over the controls of the new institutions — at a dead run.

The adult and youth components of environmental education are not mutually exclusive. Indeed, they must not be. During the decade of transition, environmental education must facilitate interaction between adult and youth, dissolve the interface between them. They must learn together, and from each other.

chapter V

environmental education

This whole book is about environmental education in its broadest sense. Up to now the emphasis has been on the adult component. Now we shift emphasis to the youth component. More specifically, environmental education — as treated in this chapter — is limited to formal school programs that make use of park and recreation resources.

Both the shift of emphasis and the limitation are artificial — for convenience. In the last two chapters I did not explicitly and systematically translate the messages of environmental management/interpretation into language and programs for young people. But this was implicit. For example, it would be hard to imagine community action without reference to and involvement of youth. Moreover, as this chapter develops, we shall see constant cross-reference between school programs and the topical matter and media of environmental management/interpretation. And we shall see also that these school programs are designed to foster interaction between young people and adults, to dissolve the distinction between the preparation-for-life student world and the real-life world of adults.

One more limitation is in order: These school programs don't make teachers out of park and recreation personnel. The resource is used as a classroom. Resource personnel aid and complement the activities of teachers and students in that classroom, but they don't take over the teaching function. The reasons for this are many: Teaching is a profession and art with its own canons, demands, and skills; therefore it is best to leave teaching to teachers. Further, park and recreation personnel don't have time to be teachers. If they take time, their impact on environmental education will be limited to very few classes, instead of spread out — through multiplier-effect management and organization — to many classes. Finally, the teacher using a park or recreation resource for environmental education — as distinct from an old-style field trip — has to be in the thick of it, or there will be no carry-over back to the school itself. This necessity poses two inhibitions: The interpreter whose knowledge of the resource makes him feel sorry for, or superior to, the teacher must control his impulse to take over; and the teacher who would gladly let the interpreter carry the ball can't be allowed to do so.

With these ground rules behind us, let us now get a fix on environmental education itself.

What are the objectives of environmental education? In most basic terms, these objectives are to involve the student in natural processes so that he understands his part in and dependence on them; to bring him to awareness of the social processes that impinge upon natural processes; to motivate creation within himself of an environmental ethic, and, finally, to activate his ethics-based concern. In this process he comes to understand that man/man relationships are as important as man/environment relationships in achieving a healthy total environment.

Implicit in this set of objectives is an important corollary: The student's concern over the big picture of environmental crisis and needed reform must be matched by opportunities for immediate environmental-reform expression and action — else the problem becomes overwhelming and kills the motivation for constructive involvement. This "brighten the corner where you are" approach opens the door for students to practice environmental reform on their own scale of operation — to experience the feeling, through action, that they *can* be a determining force in shaping the future, rather than passive victims.

Environmental education mirrors the educational objectives treated in previous chapters. Adjustments are made to accommodate formal educational settings and methodology, but the ends sought are the same.

If we are to help students and teachers exploit our resources for environmental education purposes, we must know something of their world. They, too, operate within structured systems reflecting historical missions and modes. They, too, must find ways to break traditional patterns, change them into vehicles for environmental education. And they, too, face controversy and risk as they struggle through the transition from yesterday's societal consensus to the new one emerging from environmental crisis.

Traditionally, education has been society's instrument for socializing young people. Its job has been to convert varieties of young people — the products of differential nature and nurture — into basically similar adults. Education, then, makes good citizens. People who endorse society's values, live within its rules, and contribute to its perpetuation are good citizens. All of this assumes a body of commonly held doctrine about society and its values and what constitutes good citizenship.

But today society, the value systems that define it,

and the citizenship that embodies it, take on different meanings for different people. Now is a time when new definitions struggle with old ones, a time when new doctrines develop to meet the new conditions spawned by environmental crisis. In such a world being an educator is difficult. If society splits down the middle, if value systems are in flux, if good citizenship means many things, then education looses its moorings. It lacks a common doctrine to instill.

Doesn't all this sound vaguely familiar? Of course it does! The education profession treads new ground these days, just as we do. And the common bonds of stress and aspiration can help forge joint effort. For teachers, as for park and recreation people, the basic rationale for jumping into the lifeboat and pulling full weight at the oars is the same: It simply has to be done or life will be lost. And, in a very special way, educators can't escape the obligation. Since education is society's incubator, it would be wrong if educators did not convey to students the why's and wherefore's of society's present travail. It is the essence of good citizenship that students prepare themselves to speed the transition to better days.

Beyond these matters of controversy, risk, and moral obligation, the schools face problems similar to ours at the level of resources and mechanics — people and money already committed within a frame of established curricula, textbooks, schedules, and test requirements. By understanding these limitations we can better use our resources and skills to assist teachers.

Despite the fact that new ideas on environmental education are brewing at the national and state levels, most school systems, administrators, and teachers are starting from scratch. How can you individually be helpful — in a way that goes beyond a simple offer of your resource for environmental education purposes?

As a starter, you can participate with school administrators and teachers in developing an environmental education framework. Within a school or school system you can join with committed people, reinforcing them to create a climate for innovative environmental education. A general outline of "getting-started" procedure will be useful, subject to variations that work for you and your school clientele.

First, assuming that the school system near you has a few gung ho environmentalists, you can identify and work with this cadre. *They* should choose an environmental education coordinator to act as spokesman and liaison, both within the school system and with you. The coordinator's job is to refine environmental education potentials, based on your resource, and then present them as specific projects that the administration and school board can evaluate and support.

Second, upon getting initial support from administrators and the school board, the cadre should work with you to set up workshops that bring teachers and administrators to your resource. These workshops help individual teachers relate their experience, teaching specialties, and curriculum requirements to the environmental education potentials of the park or recreation resource. As teachers explore these potentials they will begin to see the possibilities for curriculum-integrated, multi-disciplinary teaching approaches. It is important that school administrators join in these workshops, for their cooperation will be essential in helping teachers develop a coordinated environmental education program.

Third, on the basis of the educators' exposure to your personnel and physical resources, mutually agreeable starts can be made. Selected teachers and classes can experiment with your area or facility as an environmental education laboratory. You, knowing their needs, can provide teacher aids and, within limits that respect your on-going operational requirements, make personnel available to complement the school program.

Fourth, through participation in PTA meetings, parents' nights, and other public-contact events, you can help educators inform the community of the why's, what's, and how's of environmental education. These beginnings open the gate that will help your school community develop a full-scale environmental education program. In this field, as in other phases of environmental communications/reform/action, park and recreation people and resources serve as catalysts. The basic objective of your involvement is to give the schools and the community a place to start.

¶ Ideally, environmental education should be a co-ordinated progression. Curriculum-integrated and multi-disciplinary, it should move from preschool through college and graduate school, and then be followed by formal and informal adult education. Curriculum proposals at the national level and in many states (California, Michigan, and New York, among others) indicate that such comprehensive approaches may soon be the norm across the nation. Meanwhile, each school and school system can begin now to approximate this ideal.

The overall design for environmental education is of paramount importance to a comprehensive program. This design, hinging on *concepts, stages, inquiry method*, and *settings*, is described in the pages that follow.

Certain fundamental *concepts* pervade environmental education, whatever the subject-matter vehicle:

The world is finite, a closed system.

The world is not only for mankind, but must be shared with something like 5 million other kinds of living things.

Man, though the world's dominant species, is not exempt from nature.

Every organism uses a proportionate part of its surroundings; but overuse kills the system.

The earth is a system composed of a series of systems; there are relationships within systems and between systems; good systems have the flexibility that allows change, yet the stability for long life.

The principles of ecology allow man to understand the world system, of which he is a part.

Man neither creates nor destroys anything; he only changes things — thus he cannot dispose of anything.

No system is static; there is constant change.

When man changes a particular part of his surroundings, his act affects other parts of the environment; the degree or massiveness of man's acts determines the scope of environmental impact.

Every system has a buffering or carrying capacity, which is finite as to the shocks it can take, the insults it can absorb, the population it can sustain.

In sum, the world ecosystem must be viewed as a commons; any individual or individual species that overuses the commons may be richer in the short run, but in the long run all of life is poorer on the average.

Based on understanding of these principles, man can adjust his population and his derivative social systems to fit the requirements of viability of basic natural systems.[1]

The *stages* of environmental education provide a functional sequence for student exposures and experiences:

Stage One functions as a bridge, taking the child from his home milieu, where man calls the shots and nature is simply a taken-for-granted backdrop, to a milieu where nature calls the shots and man is a visitor.

The first essence of environmental awareness is knowledge of something so simple, and yet so profound — and so obscured by man's attitudes and constructs — that most people haven't even thought of it: The world doesn't need man. It runs quite well on its own.

Until this profound perspective becomes an integral part of a person's world view, that person will be unable to escape the false attitude that nature exists for the convenience of man. Until this attitude is seen as a myth, mankind will continue to act on the assumption that man's proper business is the "control of nature." In reality, the very opposite is true. Nature controls man. Nature is antecedent to man, as is the mother to the child. Nature is a total system encompassing all of its parts, including man. Nature's laws are the ultimate laws, and man, along with all other species, is subject to them. Until students are given opportunity to discover this reality, they cannot relate validly to the rest of the world.

From conception to birth, the human fetus recapitulates the history of man's biological evolution. It begins as a single cell, then becomes fishlike, then like a

---

[1] Above concepts and ecological principles paraphrased from "Ecological Principles as a Part of General Education," by Dr. John H. Thomas, Department of Biological Science, Stanford University. Dr. Thomas delivered this paper in Portland, Oregon, in May 1970, at the Environmental Science Conference for State Supervisors of Science.

lower mammal, and finally it assumes human form. Figuratively, environmental education recapitulates man's socio-cultural evolution within nature's womb: a world without man; then early man getting a tentative foothold in the life community; then the swift evolution that began with agriculture and led to modern technological man. Stage One of the environmental education process takes children back to dawn times to see how much a part of nature they really are.

Stage Two deals with man the tool-wielding manipulator of the physical environment. All of the questions in this stage stem from this very basic one: What is the relationship between man's *assumptions* about the world and his place in it, and the *facts* about the world and man? Answers to this question, in all its variations, are found in the consequences of man's acts. At this point man ceases to be a single entity and becomes the many families of man — each family (or culture) identified by its own set of assumptions and acts and consequences.

Historically, some cultures have conformed to nature's laws. That is to say, their assumptions about the world and man's place in it squared with the facts about the world and man. Their acts produced consequences that did not disrupt the natural order. Other cultures, their assumptions at odds with the facts, disrupted the natural order. Despite the homogenizing influence of world-wide technology, some men *still* try to live harmoniously within the natural order, obedient to its laws. Others, ignorant or disdainful of the natural order, destroy it.

The essence of Stage Two is exposure to another major perspective — another simple but profound notion: Different cultures have evolved *alternate value systems* by which they have ordered *their* relationships with the *natural order*. This understanding has its corollary: Judged by the health of social and physical environments, some value systems work and some don't.

Stage Three capitalizes on the notion of alternate value systems. Simply, value systems determine acts, acts determine consequences, consequences determine the kind of world that men live in. *The student now knows that the natural order is basic, that man is derivative of that order. He knows that nature's laws are constant, that man's laws can vary.*

With these perspectives the student is equipped to conceptualize a future in which man — the derivative, the variable — can adapt himself to that which is basic and constant. He can visualize social processes as a key, the natural order as a pre-existing lock. Reading the structure and the processes of the lock, he can cut the key to fit. This conception is a philosophical world view, not a detailed plan. The natural order is flexible enough to accommodate many keys — many versions of the good life. But all variances must respect the basic tolerance of the lock.

Now the student has a basis for judging the acts flowing from the social processes that surround him, of which he is a part. Now he is ready to translate his understanding into action: Those acts that conserve or regenerate the total environment, he can endorse. Those acts whose consequences would disrupt the environment, he can challenge. And in the great gray area where consequences appear dubious or are unknown, he can insist upon environmental evaluation *before* the causative acts are allowed to occur.

The stages of environmental education break through culturally induced illusions and assumptions that heretofore shaped the student's view of the world. They give him fresh perspectives of nature, of man, of the future. From this fresh base he can discern what is real and constant, what is illusory and temporal. He can balance true necessity against the false necessities of cultural lag. *He can choose for himself.*

All stages of the environmental education process require a balanced involvement that taps the student's intellectual, sensory, and emotional attributes. Cold operational knowledge is not enough. The complexity and the subtle relationships illustrated by natural phenomena spur the admiration of the intellect. Textures, patterns, smells, and sounds — the play of light and shadow on running water and tumbling waves — these stimulate the senses. The beauty, the strength, the fragility, the uniqueness of life — these open the heart to love and companionship.

Indeed, the soul of understanding lies in the human capacity for appreciation and wonder. Nature's moods and harmonies and mysteries reside within each student, for, as a part of nature, he is their product. Environmental education must plumb these depths — to help the student reactivate the natural being in himself.

Social processes have conspired to insulate all of us from the natural world of which we are a part. A revised treatment of that world — and of each other — hinges on regeneration of that part of our souls atrophied by insulation and disuse. Only then can we revere the natural world and love our partners in life. Only then can we cross the artificial threshhold that locks us out of the natural world. And only then can we conceive the ethical basis for constructive citizenship on the good ship earth.

The *inquiry method*, the third element of environmental education's conceptual design, starts with questions. The teacher's role (like the interpreter's) is not to give the answers but to create a context — through evidence, discussion, and discovery — that motivates students to their own conclusions. If the topic is the human ecology of providing food for increasing populations, one question would certainly relate to the recent development of plant hybrids and agricultural techniques that massively increase crop yields. What are the pro's and con's of this "green revolution"? Getting answers to this question would involve much conflicting evidence. Ecologists would stress the detrimental effects of heavy doses of chemicals on the soil. Agronomists would tout the potential for feeding mass populations. Demographers would assert that increased crop yields buy only a little time in the race between food production and people production. Out of this mix of evidence, students would discover that the green revolution is no panacea; it can give the world a little more time to institute effective birth-control measures, but even that time will be bought dearly in terms of soil damage.

From these initial conclusions students could draw up their own versions of environmental principles, such as "There are no free lunches in environmental affairs — mankind always pays a price for altering natural processes." In this case, are the *social* benefits worth it? And so on.

Settings help students develop an environmental philosophy through *encounters* with people, institutions, places, and media. A few exemplary *settings*, adjusted to grade level, are presented to serve as models and analogs. Based on them, you and the teachers you work with can inventory the local scene and select your own environmental encounters.[2]

For basic setting model we use the National Environmental Study Area (NESA) program developed by the National Park Service in cooperation with the Office of Education and other agencies and organizations. This model is chosen for a number of reasons: It is designed specifically for school programs that make use of park and recreation resources (with application to such urban facilities as museums, zoos, aquariums, botanical gardens, community centers, and libraries),

---

[2] Dr. William B. Stapp, Associate Professor, School of Natural Resources, The University of Michigan, has developed the concept of environmental encounters in the Fall 1970 issue of *Environmental Education*, pp. 35-41.

and it is complemented by a parallel program, the National Environmental Education Development (NEED) which provides interdisciplinary education materials for school use. Most importantly, a guide to study area use is readily available for immediate application at your resource by way of a published guide booklet developed by the National Park Service and published by the National Education Association.[3]

With this booklet in hand you can approach school administrators and teachers with a coherent plan of action for environmental education. Instructions are given for selecting and operating ESA's (which can be defined as designated settings for environmental encounters), organizing schools for environmental education, and conducting community relations.

A National Park Service folder aimed at teachers gives a quick overview of the NESA concept.[4]

> NESAs provide a different kind of environmental learning experience that makes imaginative use of both the cultural and natural worlds, as they combine to make up the study areas. The areas, together with the study guide materials developed for the area and the regular school curriculum, help students relate to their world by:
>
> 1. Introducing them to their total environment — cultural and natural, past and present.
> 2. Developing in them an understanding of how man is using his resources.
> 3. Equipping them to be responsible and active members of the world they are shaping and being shaped by.
>
> Some NESAs are primarily natural. In them are exemplified the elements and forces and balances out of which man himself is made and out of which he spins his cities and society and culture. Everything man is, or builds,

---

3 *Man and His Environment, An Introduction to Using Environmental Study Areas,* National Education Association, Washington, D.C., 1970.

4 Copies of the NESA folder are available from The Director, National Park Service, U.S. Dept. of the Interior, Washington, D.C. 20240.

is "nature" before it is anything else.

Other NESAs are primarily cultural. Their cultural significance generally springs from certain natural factors . . . a rise of ground that formed a logical battlefield, or a desirable landing site along a river that grew into a gateway to some interior region. In such places, a youngster learns to recognize how the environment has affected man's development. The environment and the individual become an indivisible whole — a reality whose meaning for each person lies in his own involvement.

*   *   *

The goal of the NESA program is a personal environmental ethic, based on an understanding of the earth's life support systems and how they work.

The first stage in achieving this goal is environmental literacy. An environmentally literate person is one who understands that he is an inseparable part of a system composed of people, culture and the natural environment.

He accepts the fact that man's activities alter the interrelationships of this system.

He grasps the implications of the human ability to consciously manipulate, control, wisely use, preserve, or destroy his environment.

He possesses a fundamental knowledge of the problems confronting man and of ways he can act toward solving these problems.

As he acquires environmental literacy, he develops a personal environmental ethic; he adjusts his own personal set of attitudes and life style to this new understanding; he assumes responsibility for the condition of his environment; he is motivated to do something about it.

The child who would achieve environmental literacy must realize that he, himself, is as much a part of the natural world — as subject to its laws — as are the trees, the mountains and the seas . . .

Teacher workshops, set up through the sponsoring resource agencies and carried out in cooperation with the local school system, introduce teachers to the NESA, provide resource material on the area, and suggest ways of adapting the on-site experience to the entire range of classroom curriculum.

At the workshops, emphasis is placed on interpretation of regular curriculum through the use of the five dynamic strands. Successful operation of this process enables a child to see the relationships that exist throughout the universe — from the farthest galaxy to his own living room. The NESA Guide supplies the information on the strands and related material, the workshops show the teachers how to use them, and the teachers themselves decide how best to fit them into the daily curriculum flow.

Environmental Strands are tools for finding relationships. Teachers and students use them to *discover why* things are as they are. That way they don't get hung up on the taxonomic, what-is-it brand of nature study. The discovery context assures involvement of students because they must actively apply themselves to figure out why; not sit back and listen to answers rattled off by the teacher. It encourages students to discover *the big idea* of unity.

These descriptions of *environmental strands*, from *Man and His Environment*,[5] give a feeling for the *big idea* approach:

I   VARIETY AND SIMILARITIES: Many likenesses and differences occur among living and non-living things. A variety of functions, sizes, and structures exist in plants and stars, rocks and animals, processes and people. However, there are sufficient similarities to permit you to classify them into orderly patterns. These classifications increase your understanding of your world.

II   PATTERNS: Organizational patterns are kinds of structures which may be found in such things as rock formations as well as in social groups of people and animals. Functional patterns include traffic movements and classroom schedules. Spatial arrangements are patterns that often please us. We find such patterns both in nature and in artistic design.

---

5 *Man and His Environment*, p. 23.

III   INTERACTION AND INTERDEPENDENCE: Nothing exists in isolation. You are constantly interacting with living and non-living things: your family, your books, your friends, your world. These people and things also depend on you in order to function properly. The process is continuous (as part of the life cycle) even after death, for dead life-forms nourish the living.

IV   CONTINUITY AND CHANGE: Both living and non-living things are constantly changing — whether among galaxies and planets or your body cells and body systems. Some things remain the same in spite of change. Matter and energy may change in form, but they can never be created or destroyed.

V   EVOLUTION AND ADAPTATION: Over centuries upon centuries of time, living and non-living things alter and develop in the process we call evolution. Probably the greatest number of changes over the longest periods of time are brought about in order to "fit" the environment. Hereditary factors then preserve the elements that are continuing. The characteristics that enable us to fit (adapt) best (for example, the best food-finder) are apt to be the traits passed on from generation to generation and insure survival of the species.

Though the environmental study area concept emphasizes outdoor environmental education at designated sites, the principle can be adapted and applied anyplace — outdoors or indoors, whether a set-aside geographic area or not: a classroom, a schoolyard, a garbage dump (ESA's show not only pristine nature but also man's impact, good or bad), a ranch, a parking lot, a mine, a construction site, a reservoir, a slum tenement, an airport, a freeway, a factory — you name it.

Now assuming that the mechanics are under control, that schools and teachers are ready to begin, let's visit some settings — whether called ESA's or something else — and put the principles of environmental education to work.

These scenarios and examples give a shotgun impression of environmental education potentials — through a variety of settings and combinations. Some of them are adaptable to your resource. Others center on the school or community. They could very well be extended applications of environmental education experiences and exposures gained at your resource, which illustrates the multiplier-effect of environmental education activities at park and recreation resources: to inspire carry-over back to the school, the neighborhood, the community. Such carry-over should result not only in community-founded environmental education facilities. It should also help the people of the community gain a new perspective on the community itself — as a place where environmental education and reform become real-life adventures in the daily lives of young people *and* adults.

A subsidiary purpose in presenting this catalogue of settings is to give you ammunition to pass on to teachers. When they say, "Sure, I want to start environmental education, but what kinds of things can I do?", you have, in what follows, a few answers.

First stop is the Environmental Study Area at Bandelier National Monument, New Mexico. The setting is the canyon of the Rito de los Frijoles, which descends from the Pajarito Plateau to the Rio Grande. It is an ideal place to apply the environmental strands, as the following selections from the teacher workbook demonstrate:

BIG IDEAS

Identification of plants and animals as to species is *not* important to this program. What is important is that you and the students become more aware of the natural world, the undisturbed environment. We will be concerned with sounds, smells, interactions and relationships, in nature.

Examples

Area One. On the downstream trail to the meadows.

1. After rising above the stream, note the demarcation between dense stream-side vegetation and sparse slope-and-cliff vegetation.

Varieties and similarities, illustrated by a variety of plant types with similar basic needs, but in different physical environments. *Patterns,* illustrated by relative density of plant populations. *Interaction and interdependence,* illustrated by the common denominator of *water,* and its relative availability.

Continuity and change, shown in the transition zone (intermixture) between the two ecosystems.

Evolution and adaptation, shown by the ability of pinyon and juniper to survive on dry slopes (as opposed to stream-hugging cottonwoods).

2. A blow-down area, with rotting logs replenishing the soil.

Continuity and change . . .

Interaction and interdependence . . .

3. Lichen-covered rocks

Interaction and interdependence (symbiosis).

*　　　*　　　*

6. Broad-leaf (water-loving) trees extending up slope in deeper ravines (equals more shade and concentrated water supply from funneled runoff).

Adaptation . . . (to a very particular terrain feature).

7. Erosion-loosened rocks on talus slopes below cliffs.

Continuity and change . . .

8. Moss taking over a lichen rock. (Lichens create a moist net on otherwise barren rock; moisture-loving moss can then "move in.")

Interaction and interdependence . . .

9. Animal tracks and droppings on trail. (Examine droppings and find what animals ate; what kind of animal eats . . .?)

Interaction and interdependence . . .

Evolution and adaptation . . .

10. In drier pinyon-juniper areas, predominance of juniper — why, because juniper can "take it" better where it's drier.

Evolution and adaptation . . .

11. Different plant radii on slopes vs. flats. (Sparser plant growth on slopes because of less water.)

Interdependence (on water supply)

Adaptation . . .

*   *   *

20. Park-like meadows with ponderosa pines (field trip objective). This area is very fragile in places. Set up test area to demonstrate fragility — children interact with this environment to sense their presence in it.

Interaction and interdependence . . . (between children and their environment of the moment — the here and now).

Area Two. On upstream trail to environmental study area.

21. Oak trees within a circle of towering ponderosas all lean toward the one break in the circle (where a rock outcrop bars the ponderosas). Great example of phototropism. Even on a warm day, this shady grove is cool —

kids will move to a sunny spot, too, just as the oaks seek it — we are phototropic like trees . . .

Adaptation . . .

*   *   *

23. Abert squirrels in the ponderosa pines. (This squirrel lives almost exclusively on ponderosa seeds; therefore not found away from this species of tree.)

Interaction and interdependence . . .

Evolution and adaptation . . .

24. The school area is a place of rich stream ecology. Of special interest is the plant called Horsetail (*Equisetum*). This plant grows only in silica-rich soil that is well watered. It can take or leave sunlight if it has silica and water. Thus it can be found in sunny, downstream areas, or in cool shady areas far upstream. Children can take samples of this fascinating plant, which, because of its tough, silica substance is also known as scouring rush.

Evolution and adaptation . . .

The upstream school area (which includes wide ponderosa-covered benches along the trail) is attractive for two other specific reasons: Erosion of cliffs, high up and at stream level, with much oxidation and seepage of mineral elements, has produced exquisite patterns and colors that are naturals for artistic expression. Also, many small coves in the cliffs are directly exposed to sunlight; here grow desert plants (yucca, cactus). These enclaves of the desert, far up in a canyon that is mainly Canadian, in terms of life zone, produce a weird effect.

Summing up.

The environmental school at Bandelier should give any teacher an infinitude of opportunities to use the strands within the context of the child's interests and sensory explorations. Discoveries are at every turn of the trail. Living things — plant and animal — abound in great variety and interesting interrelationship. The designated school areas are large enough and diverse enough to provide both field trip variety and "quiet hour" privacy.

The workshop leads the teacher into this place of discovery. Using the strand clues she learns how to read the processes and relationships exhibited by the ESA. Based on her own experience, she then uses the clues as starting points for her students.

What happens to children in this kind of environment? They burst to express themselves — in art, in language, in joy. Here are poems written by fifth-grade children who discovered much about themselves as they discovered the Bandelier ESA:

Bubbles

One of the most beautiful sights to me
Are the bubbling bubbles in front of me
They run through the stream without a care
And you can see them everywhere.
You never know what they will say.
They bang against the rocks and trees,
And during winter they will freeze.

Karen Day

Sounds I Hear

The sounds that I hear,
Are pleasing to my ear.
The wind whistling through the trees,
The sound of the buzzing bees.
The stream rushing in and out,
Whispering secrets on its route.
All of these, and many more,
Are mine to share on the forest floor.

Kathy Bearden

Why I Would Like Bandelier for My Home

*I would like Bandelier for my home instead
of the city. The air is so fresh; the flowing
streams are beautiful; the canyons are too
grand to describe.*

*The traffic is not so great or swift to keep
you frightened.*

*These are reasons I would like to make Bandelier
my home.*

Patty Rost

Hiakus

*Spring is here to stay
Summer is so far away
Fall may never come.*

*Branches disappear
Leaves in the little stage
Green leaves fill the air.*

Jim Sauer

At another ESA children spent a day at an historic
pioneer cabin. In costume and material effects they
recreated pioneer life. They carried water from a spring,
made their own fire, cooked their own bread. For them
the ESA was a time machine. It took them back to days
when people spent most of their time and energy just
hustling for necessities, in an environment with few
conveniences, where no favors were granted.

At the middle grade level, ESA's may concentrate on the impact of technological man upon the environment. For example, Mission Bay Park in San Diego illustrates the full gamut — from pristine nature to man-caused degradation (Mission Bay became a foul-smelling garbage dump) to man-caused rejuvenation (through environmental management the community restored Mission Bay as a park and water recreation area).

A reservoir recreation area in Oklahoma has instituted an Environmental Study Tour, which brings together a mosaic of mini-ESA's: a dam here, an abandoned mine there, road construction over here, reclaimed farm land over there. Each site illustrates a pro or a con in environmental management, sometimes both. For example, the dam is earthen. Its retaining bank has been carefully sodded to prevent erosion. That's a good mark. But near the dam, where the earth fill was excavated, erosion guts the valley and silts the stream. That's a bad mark. The contrast illustrates a narrow kind of environmental management. Men took care of the dam, but they didn't give a care about the quarry site — because it was of no functional value to them. Of course the folks downstream have a different way of looking at it!

Environmental encounters are everywhere. The notion that environmental education and *nature study* are synonyms is flat wrong. Settings are where you happen to be. And the strands work as well in urban settings as rural and wild ones.

So it's off to the city, and to the setting most familiar to students . . .

The classroom is where it all begins: a teacher, some students, and the abiding urge to understand and be effective in this world. Often, because of budget limitations and restrictive rules, the classroom will be just about it, in terms of place. But with the aid of people, institutions, and media, the world can be squeezed into the classroom. Anyway, the classroom itself is an environment. Let's take these two aspects of the classroom — itself an environment, a microcosm of the world; and, by way of imports, a repository of the world out there — and use them as bases for environmental encounters in the primary grades.

These students spend lots of time in this classroom. They must have some opinions about it — as an environment that closes them in for some hours each day. A basic technique in environmental education — as in all other kinds — is to have the students themselves structure their environmental encounters.

What, in this room, is pleasing or displeasing — as the children see it? How might they emphasize the one, de-emphasize the other? What are the possibilities for artistic embellishment of the physical environment of this room? How might poetry, or a song, or the arrangement of desks and tables smooth the social processes?

Why not start by having the children inventory the physical aspects of the room, and the social processes that go on there? Then they could express their views on what is good and what is bad. This identifies problems. Problems cry for solution. What are the children's solutions? And how can they organize and discipline themselves to accomplish them? This leads to revised social processes, based on leadership, skills and imagination.

The children may have a window in their room. Maybe they want to face it instead of the blackboard. What are the pro's and con's of this? Evaluation develops the concept of environmental costs and benefits. Maybe they *could* face the window at certain times!

Is the heat too high? The air too stuffy? Could the janitor be invited in to hear a student petition on this matter? This calls for tact and good community relations.

Meanwhile, this environmental encounter — where the children live, not out there — has used every attribute, every skill the children possess. They have observed their classroom world. In response to the stimuli it offers, they have expressed their feelings and their opinions in art, in language, in music, in mathematics. They have experienced social interaction amongst themselves, with their teacher, and with at least some members of the extended school community.

Most important, they get experience in questioning the "givens" of their world and choosing an environment, a future, more to their liking. They have become active participants in the world's work. Environmental education *is* education for life.

Before dropping this idea, let's extend its principle beyond this primary classroom. How many new schools have you seen recently? If they are like most new schools, architecture has used up the construction budget and landscaping has been forgotten or been an afterthought — known as the sprinkle-some-grass-seed syndrome. Bare, buffeted by wind-blown dust, the schoolyard — the context of education for life — is a travesty of quality environment. In some schools students organize themselves — and the community — to rectify such environmental mismanagement. They enlist their parents and their parents' friends in this effort. A landscape architect draws up a landscape plan. A nurseryman contributes plantings. The students raise money by collecting paper, aluminum, and other "waste" to be recycled into the production system — which shows how one environmental reform objective can be hitched up to another. Community work days bring students and parents together *to do something about* their community environment — as symbolized by the schoolyard.

Now back to the primary classroom — this time as a setting through which the world "out there" parades.

For years teachers have imported the world into their classrooms, using people, institutions, and media. Now, they consciously seek out environmentalists and environmental orientations for such activities. Park and recreation people can help teachers get started in this direction by serving on speakers' bureaus and by encouraging other agencies and businesses to participate.

Let's move out of the classroom and take a tour of the community. Kids like some things, don't like others. Here we have the beginnings of an environmental inventory of this community. In some places this sort of experience has been the germ of an environmental essay contest — which could involve the whole school, the whole community.

Is there a local museum, a library, a town hall? Could this be the place where community leaders might assemble to hear selected essays and see supporting art work, to judge these efforts and bestow prizes? All answers are yes.

Adults might be surprised at the sensitivity of their youngsters. They might even be moved to improve their community to meet the high standards of children mercifully unconfused by zoning ordinances, politically inspired variances therefrom, and the "practical" arguments of economics!

Enlisting participation of community leaders and institutions will take some work. Logistics of the tour, arrangements for presentation night, and provision of prizes (which should have an environmental twist, like a paid family vacation to a park or recreation area) will require public and school-administration cooperation. So the community's participation should be at the sponsorship level to grease the skids for the teacher and the kids. How about a sponsoring coalition of park and recreation people, along with supporting conservation and business groups? Here, as always, the lines cross between environmental education and environmental management. The education of participating adults is as important in this setting as the education of young people. The essay-contest evaluation of the community puts adult managers of the community on the spot — to save face with their kids. And, repetitive truism that it is, the general community environment sets the tone for park and recreation environments.

Many's the game that can be played in this essay contest. For example, one child might write his essay from the viewpoint of an ancient Indian or explorer who has, Rip Van Winkle-like, returned to this time and place ("When I first came here . . . Now I see . . ."). Another could take an artist's view. Another, a scientist's. Another could be a businessman. Another, the mayor. Another, a playground superintendent, or customer. Another, someone who likes to ride her bicycle downtown, or walk from place to place without getting killed on the freeway. Another, a patient with respiratory illness. And so on. (This principle of putting on different glasses can be used in many contexts and activities.)

Another angle on the essay contest (and related activities) is to take advantage of already-existing institutional programs. A museum may be sponsoring an environmental film festival, a library or college an environmental lecture series, a park an environmental forum. It would be a simple matter to schedule these public events to complement the essay contest.

Community tours are not new, nor are the community resources that teachers have traditionally used. The viewpoint and the mode of use *are* new. Before teachers take their children to a zoo, or a museum, or a botanical garden, or an aquarium, they should do some pre-tour prepping. The point today is not simply to see a mountain lion, an Indian diorama, a tree, or a trout, but to get the zoologist, the curator, the botanist, or the guy who knows about fish to explain the environmental implications of the seeing experience. What does it take for a mountain lion to live? Are there still some environments around that meet these conditions? How come people still get paid to kill mountain lions, and is it good to do this? Prehistoric pots and weaving say things about people in their environment. For example, the ancient Pueblos could make it in places where modern men would starve — *because* they knew every last thing about their environment and its products, and they knew how to tread lightly when they used the environment instead of tearing it up the way we do. Trees die when they breathe too much carbon monoxide. What's that mean for people? Just how clean should a stream be to support trout — and kids who want to swim?

At the upper-grade level, environmental education becomes reform-action oriented. It explores the interaction of social and natural processes — and it lets the chips fall where they may. The final scenario demonstrates this point, and it makes clear the meaning of curriculum integration. It bears repeating that environmental education is *not* an added subject to be crammed into already crowded curricula and schedules. It is, rather, a philosophic context that contains and influences extant teaching-learning patterns. Look upon it as an injection that breaks down walls between subject-matter pigeon-holes, then integrates them for common purpose. Each subject contributes to environmental insights, and, by relating to other subjects, reinforces their capacity to carry part of the environmental load. Now let us translate this nebulous concept into a working example:

A current events class tackles the problem of denatured, chemically adulterated foods (remember the flap over non-nutritional dry cereals?). Using the inquiry method, teacher and students probe the reasons why eating the breakfast of chumps kept Jack Armstrong out of the Olympics. In the course of inquiry the history of agriculture and food supply in an urbanizing America momentarily takes center stage. If only a few Americans on farms produce food for the great majority of city dwellers — who cannot produce food in their synthetic city environments — then farms must be highly efficient and mass productive. This means great spreads of monoculture: thousands of square miles devoted exclusively to wheat or corn. And these crops must be cultivated and harvested quickly, on precise schedules. This means mechanization of the farm.

What does this new set of farming conditions mean in ecological terms? First, monoculture is a man-caused simplification of the environment. By contrast, natural environments are complex. Many animals and plants interact, balance each other, and make specific contributions to the life process that binds living things to the soil. No one species of plant or animal can get out of hand for long, because natural limitations of food supply and predator-prey relationships continually tend toward balance — a dynamic homeostasis. But in the simplified man-made, mechanized farm environment, one crop stands alone. It takes from the soil and depletes it. No other plants replenish the soil; no draft animals spread their natural fertilizer. So chemical fertilizers have to take up the slack. When pests strike at great spreads of monoculture they meet no check from limited food supply and natural predator controls. So they "explode" and sweep vast areas (like 1970's corn blight in the Middle West). So man again introduces synthetic controls — massive pesticide spraying.

Upshot: depleted soils saturated with chemicals producing masses of food stuffs that look good but lack nutritive value and pack accumulated poisons.

As soils continue to be depleted and get "salted" from chemicals, and as pests become immune to poisons, the vicious cycle deepens and men pour more and more chemicals and poisons on. Plant products still look good, but they are chemically adulterated ghosts of natural plants.

Mechanization of farmlands drives farm workers

off the farms into the cities, for which they are ill-prepared. Unable to grow food in this new environment, lacking the talents and special adaptations necessary for city life, they fail and go on welfare. This sociological phenomenon produces the paradox of grinding poverty in the midst of affluence.

Meanwhile, the wheat and corn are processed and packaged. Chemicals are added as preservatives so that the foods can travel and sit on shelves until someone buys them. Because the basic food lacks nutrition and flavors, more chemicals are added to "enrich" them, spice their flavor, give them some oomph — turn them from synthetic paste into something palatable.

Rich and poor alike buy and eat this chemical feast. But it's worse for the poor because they can't afford proteins and other rich foods to balance out their diets. They are also largely ignorant of just how empty these adulterated foods are, even though they do ease immediate pangs of hunger. Suddenly the problem becomes one for home economics, cooking, and health classes.

We could go on proliferating this example (e.g., the basic communications and moral values of food advertising), but let us stop here and sum up. A current events headline has produced inquiry into history; into agriculture; into urbanization; into industrial, distribution, and commercial processes. It has reached into chemistry, biology, and sociology. It has posed problems of individual and public health.

That headline has opened a window on man in the web of life. It has dealt with interactions of social and natural processes. Full exploitation of this single topic would lead to questions about changing the values and processes of the food industry. It would explore the ecology of agriculture in an urbanized world. It would develop attitudinal and behavioral responses in students that would influence the home when shopping time comes. It would allow insight into the quick fatigue, lack of concentration, and poor performance of class-mates who lack the basic fuel to perform well.

In this multi-disciplinary, today-oriented environ-mental education exercise, students have gained historical and social perspectives that aid them to brush aside slogans and simplistic balderdash. They are digging at root causes. They have seen that man in the web of life is breaking strands when he breaks nature's rules, and that he, man, is the number one victim. We simply aren't talking about the esthetics of far-away places where the bird-watchers roam. We're talking about people in daily life taking the consequences of false philosophies and mistaken acts.

In terms of teaching units, this single example could spawn 50 of them. The whole school could pull together to move the results of student studies into the public arena. PTA meetings and museum exhibits could be platforms for a larger educational program. This would involve art and manual arts and public speaking and research in many fields. Local colleges could be tapped for expert speakers at such school-sponsored programs. Making this kind of public education project go would throw students into the crucible of in-the-system environmental action. They would deal with local media, consumer organizations, food outlets. They would seek information from government agencies in the public health and regulatory fields. In the process they would learn where are the strong and weak points of our social processes. Who in their community is letting whom get away with what. Who is fighting the good environmental fight, and who is the opposition. The complexity and indefatigable labors of turning a society around would strike home quickly. Illusions about idealized "civics" would be replaced by tough understandings about the world and what it takes to change it for the better. The reform impatience that flames brilliantly, then wanes into disillusionment and drop-out, would be transmuted to dogged, long-term durability.

At this point, I'm dropping the scenario style in favor of brief *Item* references to exemplary environmental education activities.

Item: Middle- or upper-grade students perform environmental survey of their community and arrange with local newspaper, radio, and TV outlets to report their findings, including photographic documentation. (Photography club, art class, debate society, dramatics club — all of these groups should take part.)

Item: Students petition library (museum, college, etc.) to inaugurate Environmental Bookshelf, public education programs.

Item: Students isolate socio-economic problem in community and join in political action to rectify it (e.g., poor community services "across the tracks," as they say). Action *includes* presentations before city council and the planning commission.

Item: Same for specific public health problem.

Item: Same for environmental management of community (waste disposal practices, water pollution from industry, construction standards, park needs, etc.). Add the twist of a student-sponsored public forum with government, academia and conservation-group participation.

Item: Students set up environmental clearinghouse for community where citizens can get information on air and water pollution, trash recycling, environmental poisons (mercury, pesticides, detergents), food adulterants, noise pollution, and so on.

Item: Students man environmental early warning system so that concerned citizens have someplace to report nascent problems before they blow up into crisis. Students relay information to proper authorities (with an "insurance" copy to local conservation organization).

¶ The potential is endless. The inter-disciplinary mix crosses all lines — nobody is solving anything these days when he says, "It's not in my department." Students get out of the old-fashioned context where education-is-preparation-for-life and jump into a new context where education *is* life.

Every community needs all the help it can get to deal with its environmental problems. Why always pick on the old retired volunteers? Just because kids can't work, in the job-holding sense, doesn't mean that they should be cut out of community life altogether. You'd be frustrated, too, if you were a supernumerary in your society — if you were always in the process of *becoming*, instead of *being* right here and now — if school were a place where you were held in limbo just about long enough to let your ideals and enthusiasms cool and disappear. Environmental education, properly conceived, puts students into the mainstream where the action is.

Public education in American has always aimed to give students the motivation and the tools with which to realize themselves and contribute to the welfare of society at large. In this sense, the objectives of environmental education are not new. What *is* new is the world that technological man has wrought. His impact on the physical environment threatens the conditions that allow quality life. Environmental education meets this threat by showing students that their chances for the good life depend upon the existence of a healthy physical environment. It aids them to discover the natural laws that man must obey to perpetuate a healthy physical environment. It helps them to envision a society that conforms to these laws. And, finally, it challenges students to begin shaping such a society *now.*

interlude VI

people make the future

There are two kinds of future that we don't
sufficiently discriminate between.

One is the probable future based upon the
existing institutions and agencies continuing
to act in the same way, at the same rate,
with the same impact as they have in the
past. The "probable" future is not necessarily
the actual future for all. It is always a
summary of the past, and all its predictions
are predictions about the past, not about
the future.

The other future is that based on possibility.
And instead of a strictly limited number of
probabilities, there are n number of
possibilities, some coming into existence in
an effort to modify or overcome the statistical
forecast.

Now, unfortunately, for the effect of its
predictions, science necessarily deals with
the past, either with what is known or with
what can be directly extrapolated from the
known factors. But when you concentrate upon
probabilities you are under the temptation to
take what has happened or is now happening
as an instruction for what should happen in
future. In other words, you deny yourself
possibility.

But if you understand the potentialities of
a situation, what you may learn from the past
is not that you should continue to conform to
it and to push it further and make the dominant
forces go faster, but rather that you should
stand in the way of it and oppose to it one or
another kind of future based not upon statistics,

not upon institutional inertia, but upon the
human organism itself, what its purposes and
values are. Man's autonomous decisions are
the only factors that are capable of transforming
the future. Otherwise, the future rolls on and
we roll with it or roll under it, as the case
may be.

Lewis Mumford
"Closing Statement" in
*Future Environments of
North America*, pp. 217-218.

To be autonomous, to decide upon the future, will stretch us to the limits — individually and organizationally.

What are the conditions for purposeful change?

chapter VI

the environment of change

Throughout this book I have urged you to undertake new and difficult tasks. To turn your minds around, to break out of traditional patterns and molds. This urging expressed the spirit of participants in the two Institutes on Environmental Interpretation.

On a different plane, I have tried to translate the concerns of the Institutes into functional applications for use by the park and recreation profession.

Between inspiration and application are the institutions, the groupings of people, who actually do the work. This chapter looks upon these institutions as systems that must adjust to new imperatives. As in all systems, the aim is a balance between stability and flexibility — institutional cohesion strong enough to survive controversy and innovation, but not so strong as to smother them.

Let me start with the premise that the park and recreation institutions now in being are the ones that will continue to activate the goals of this profession. There is no time to wipe the slate clean and start over with new institutions. There is no body of experienced, talented people who can march on stage and replace you. Infusions of new blood and new ideas will help. But basically we start with existing people in existing institutional arrangements. From this base the profession must evolve at revolutionary pace if it is to contribute significantly to environmental reform.

It is not the intent here to endorse change for change's sake. For years management literature, films, and conferences have been plagued by hucksters of change. Not questioning the direction of change, they worship it as something good in itself. They take what "is now happening as an instruction for what should happen in future." In fact, they urge not change at all, but simply more of the same — a compounding of what is.

Change for a purpose flows from conceptual design, which is in turn a deduction from something overriding and universal. In the context of this book, that something is the environmental imperative. The conceptual design deduced therefrom concluded Chapter II (expressed as the goals of the park and recreation profession in the environmental reform movement).

From this conceptual design, deduction took us one step further to the tactics of environmental reform: environmental management, interpretation, and education.

Deductive systems can be traps. Pure and uncluttered by operational necessity, they may be so visionary that they never jump off Cloud Nine and come down to earth. Moreover, they go against the grain of America's pragmatic, school-of-hard-knocks bias.

But inductive systems can be traps, too. (Look

about you and see the havoc they have wrought.) Constant involvement with brushfire crises and operational details tends to destroy the essential inductive leap from the particular to the general, from earth to Cloud Nine.

So we have, it would seem, another conundrum: If we begin with a vision, a universal, we may never get down to the nitty gritty needed for daily operation. If we don't step back from the busy-work of daily operation, we may never have a vision. Either course means failure.

The environment of change (constructive, purposeful change) requires synthesis: Vision infusing daily operation with purpose and discrimination; daily operation checking vision to keep it from running away with itself.

We have the materials for synthesis. The deductive system espoused by this book — a hierarchy of thought, judgment, and action descending from the overrriding environmental imperative — comprises the element of vision. This element allows us to come up for air, to judge the worth of daily actions in terms of their contribution to the future we seek, to drop those actions that don't contribute, and to devise new ones that do. The operational check resides in the existing institutional base. Its inertia is sufficient to restrain vision from over-acceleration.

What we need to balance the synthesis, to make its elements work smoothly together, is:

First: General agreement on the kind of future we seek. In the name of the environmental imperative, this book has attempted to define that future — not in detail, but in the broad frame of naturalized social processes that preserve life options.

The future we seek is one that will give us and our descendents the *choice*, i.e., the *freedom*, to experiment with many versions of the good life. This definition goes to the biological basis for choice — a healthy biosphere. Recognizing that societies evolve, that their values change, it properly defers definitions of what the good life itself should be. Concentrating on preservation of the *conditions for choice* it does not presume to *make the choice*. Deriving its direction from objective data, the instructions given to us by the biosphere, it can appeal to all rational men — whatever their subjective differences may be. It gives everyone the chance to pursue his own preferences, as long as he respects the ecological ground rules.

Second: Having agreed not to preempt the future, we must still live today. Built into management systems must be a philosophical (as distinct from technical) division of labor. This division is between the operational work force — dealing with today and immediate necessity — and the work force that renews institutions from within so that they can protect the future, i.e., preserve life options. These are the people who assure that present necessity does not foreclose future options.

This division of labor recognizes and utilizes the differences in people — people of action and peope of thought, temperaments attuned to the concrete and temporal and temperaments attuned to the abstract and timeless.

Third: Having created, through the division of labor, the potential for management systems that check and balance today against tomorrow, managers must put these counterweights to work.

The division of labor does not separate today and tomorrow. It views them as a continuum. This perspective motivates against the tendency of current management systems to discount tomorrow in favor of today. By forcing constant interaction between the divisions of labor — in both the operating and the planning contexts — managers get away from the task force syndrome, the shelves of study reports that tell us what we ought to do

— when we get organized. Managers must put tomorrow in the present, for present decisions determine what tomorrow will be.

It will be difficult, at first, for managers and their work forces to adjust to management systems that slow down action, that debate before deciding, that subject the impulses of authority to the scrutiny and the screen of objective fact.

But consider the alternative: More of the same, more of the systems of expediency that force us to bargain away the potential for life that our resources represent.

This book concludes on a personal note because its writing has been a deep personal experience. I started out in the guise of an editor-compiler, to help many readers share the inspirations of a few participants in two Institutes on Environmental Interpretation. But reading over what I have written, I realize that I have gone beyond my charter, that I have co-opted the inspirations of the Institutes for my own purposes as advocate and writer. The book has fairly synthesized the aspirations of the Institutes, it is true, but it has also been the vehicle for my own aspirations.

In the months of writing, the book became a medium for turning the frustrations of valuable experience into a positive design for the future. I have tried — honestly, without rancor — to critique the old management systems that have failed and to describe, at least in outline, the new ones that we need.

Inevitably, given such a personal experience, I have forced upon you some personal viewpoints that may rankle. But I hope that the basic message of the book is not lost for this reason. The message is that mankind must find a basis for community and shared aspiration. I know of nothing that has the ecumenical potential of the environmental imperative — not religious beliefs, not political ideologies, not the pragmatism that shifts direction with every changing breeze.

It is this message that I have tried to get across to you of the park and recreation profession — in the hope that you will buy it and propagate it, in your own way, from the resources that you manage. It is terribly important that you, in particular, do so. For your resources represent a social commitment to the sane society. In a world seemingly gone mad, such evidence of high human purpose is dear beyond any price. And the message that it signifies — about the world that could be — should be delivered remorselessly, and loud and clear.

appendix

readings and resources

The proliferation of literature, resource materials, and organizations dedicated to environmental reform deserves a major research project in its own right. I present here only a select listing of readings and resources:

- that are basic in the field

- that you can easily get or get to

- that have multiplier effects in the form of ideas, bibliographies, and guideline information.

Basic Readings

These are for your reading pleasure at the philosophical, thought-piece level.

If you want to go deep, to the foundation level of environmental insight, I recommend these two books, which are symposia tapping a broad range of disciplines and many approaches to environmental conservation. Try your library, a nearby college library, or go the library loan route to get these books, because they are expensive.

Future Environments of North America, edited by F. Fraser Darling and John P. Milton. Natural History Press, Garden City, New York, 1966.

The Subversive Science, Essays Toward an Ecology of Man, edited by Paul Shepard and Daniel McKinley. Houghton Mifflin Co., Boston, 1969.

Now for a group of paperbacks that should be in any good bookstore near you. These are classics as to the specifics they treat, and some are great literature as well.

The Forest and the Sea, Marston Bates. New American Library (Signet), 1960.

Science and Survival, Barry Commoner. Viking Press, New York, 1967.

Silent Spring, Rachel Carson. Fawcett Publications (Crest Reprint), Greenwich, Conn., 1962.

So Human an Animal, René Dubos. Charles Scribner's Sons (Lyceum Edition), New York, 1968.

The Population Bomb, Paul R. Erlich. Ballantine Books, New York,1968.

Population, Resources, Environment; Issues In Human Ecology, Paul R. and Anne H. Erlich. W. H. Freeman and Co., San Francisco, 1970.

A Sand County Almanac, Aldo Leopold. (Reprint.) Oxford University Press, New York, 1970.

America the Raped, Gene Marine. Avon Books, New York, 1969.

The Frail Ocean, Wesley Marx. Ballantine Books, New York, 1969.

Ecology, Eugene P. Odum. Holt, Rinehart and Winston, New York, 1963.

> *Moment in the Sun*, Robert and Leona Rienow. Ballantine Books, New York, 1967.
>
> *Man in the Web of Life*, John H. Storer. New American Library (Signet Books), New York, 1968.
>
> *The Quiet Crisis*, Stewart L. Udall. Avon Books, New York, 1967.

(For a more comprehensive paperback bibliography, request "It's Your World" from the Conservation Library Center, Denver Public Libary, 1357 Broadway, Denver, Colorado 80203.)

Included in the basic readings category must be the following four publications, available from the U.S. Government Printing Office, Washington, D.C. 20402. They survey national environmental problems, then describe the development steps for coherent environmental policy.

> *Restoring the Quality of Our Environment*, Report of the Environmental Pollution Panel, President's Science Advisory Committee. The White House, 1965.
>
> *Environmental Quality*, The First Annual Report of the Council on Environmental Quality. Washington, 1970.
>
> *Joint House-Senate Colloquium to Discuss a National Policy for the Environment*, Hearings before the Committee on Interior and Insular Affairs, U.S. Senate, and the Committee on Science and Astronautics, U.S. House of Representatives, 90th Cong., 2d sess., Washington, 1968.
>
> *Congressional White Paper on a National Policy for the Environment*. Washington, 1968. This White Paper is an abstract of the above-cited colloquium. Both documents are extremely valuable for clearinghouse-forum uses.

Environmental Management

As discussed in Chapter III, environmental management is as much a matter of human and institutional arrangements as it is physical manipulation of the environment. The following list of references reflects this amalgam and also provides some models of good and bad environmental management.

The political, legal, and institutional approach to environmental management is covered by these items.

Law and the Environment, edited by Malcolm Baldwin and James K. Page, Jr. A Conservation Foundation Publication. Walker and Company, New York, 1970.

Environment: A Challenge to Modern Society, Lynton Keith Caldwell. Natural History Press, New York, 1970.

The Politics of Pollution, J. Clarence Davies. Pegasus, New York, 1970.

Environment and Resources: From Conservation to Eco-management, Jaro Mayda. School of Law, The University of Puerto Rico, 1968. This excellent book uses the case study method to illustrate environmental problems and solutions in Puerto Rico — a superb exposition of the interaction of social and natural processes.

The Politics of Ecology, James Ridgeway. Dutton, New York, 1970.

Institutions for Effective Management of the Environment, Report of the Environmental Studies Board. National Academy of Sciences and National Academy of Engineering. Washington, D.C., 1970.

Environment Reporter, Bureau of National Affairs, Inc. 1231-25th St., N.W., Washington, D.C. 20037. This is one of many similar "reporter" periodicals serving professionals in the fields of environmental design, law, medicine, public health, and so on.

Models of environmental management and mismanagement can be derived from these publications.

Will Success Spoil the National Parks, Robert Cahn. *Christian Science Monitor* Reprint, Boston, 1968.

The Destruction of California, Raymond F. Dasmann. Collier Books, New York, 1966.

Man and Nature in the National Parks, Reflections on Policy, F. Fraser Darling and Noel D. Eichhorn. Conservation Foundation, Washington, D.C., 1969.

The Careless Technology: The Ecology of International Development, John P. Milton and M. T. Farvar. Natural History Press, Garden City, New York, 1971. A preview of this book appeared as a special supplement in *Natural History* magazine. Excellent case studies.

Water and Choice in the Colorado Basin: An Example of Alternatives in Water Management, Report by the Committee on Water of the National Research Council, National Academy of Sciences. Washington, D.C., 1968. Shows how scientific study of a regional entity should *precede* the setting of social and management objectives.

Publications on the philosophy of environmental planning include the following.

America's Changing Environment, Raymond Aaron, *et al.* *Daedalus*, Fall 1967.

Planning for Diversity and Change: Possible Futures and their Relation to the Man Controlled Environment, edited by S. Anderson. MIT Press, Cambridge, 1968.

Values and the Future, edited by Kurt Baier and Nicholas Rescher. The Free Press, New York, 1969.

A Different Kind of Country, Raymond F. Dasmann. Macmillan Co., New York, 1968.

Environment and Change: The Next Fifty Years and *Environment and Policy: The Next Fifty Years*, edited by William K. Ewald, Jr. Indiana University Press, Bloomington, 1967.

Redoing America: A Nationwide Report on How to Make Our Cities and Suburbs Livable, E. K. Faltermayer. Harper & Row, New York, 1968.

1976: Agenda for Tomorrow, Stewart L. Udall. Harcourt, Brace and World, Inc., New York, 1968.

In addition to references already cited in Chapter III, publications treating the esthetics and ecology of environmental manipulation include the following:

Design with Nature, Ian McHarg. Natural History Press, Garden City, New York, 1969. This is a major contribution, appealing to a broad spectrum of professionals and laymen concerned with environmental planning, design, and development. Uses case study method to illustrate social and ecological cost/benefit ratios.

Man-Made America: Chaos or Control, Christopher Tunnard and Boris Pushkarev. Yale University Press, New Haven, 1963.

The Last Landscape, William H. Whyte. Doubleday & Co., Garden City, N.Y., 1968.

Environmental Interpretation

It is difficult to come up with a specific corpus of environmental interpretation literature because all things can be interpreted environmentally — all social processes, all natural processes, and all interactions between them. Two excellent idea books are:

The Fifth Essence, Freeman Tilden. National Park Trust Fund Board, Washington, D.C., n.d. A gentle and beautiful insight into the value of quality environments.

The Dynamics of Change, Don Fabun. Prentice-Hall, Inc., Englewood Cliffs, N.J., 1967. This essay on communications in a changing world is a treasure trove of interpretive substance and technique. Fabun is editor of the Kaiser Aluminum *News.*

In addition to books listed in the basic readings, publications especially relevant to the interpretive art include:

Interpreting Our Heritage, Freeman Tilden. (Revised edition.) University of North Carolina Press, Chapel Hill, 1967.

Face of North America, Peter Farb. Harper Colophon Books, New York, 1968.

The Balance of Nature, Lorus J. and Margery Milne. Alfred A. Knopf, Inc., New York, 1960.

The Great Chain of Life, Joseph Wood Krutch. Pyramid Publications, New York, 1966.

Our Plundered Planet, Fairfield Osborn. Little, Brown and Co., Boston, 1948. An early study of man's destruction of the environment — still applicable today.

The works of Muir and Thoreau will always inspire interpreters. A modern work in the Thoreau tradition is:

The Outermost House, Henry Beston. (Reprint edition.) Viking Press, New York, 1956.

For a book attuned to juvenile understanding of the environmental imperative see:

Man, Earth and Change, Jean Worth. Coward-McCann, Inc., N.Y., 1968.

For a survey of outdoor interpretation methods in many types of sites, facilities, and jurisdictions, see:

> *Manual of Outdoor Interpretation,* edited by Joseph J. Shomon. National Audubon Society, New York, 1968.

Environmental Education

The Office of Education, U.S. Department of Health, Education and Welfare, Washington, D.C. 20202, has produced a basic packet on the rationale, methodology, and implementation of environmental education programs:

> *A New Role for American Education,* U.S. Office of Education, Washington, D.C., 1970. Request also "Readings in Environmental Awareness," a supplement of concept papers.

Helpful references for park and recreation people who are working with local schools to initiate environmental education programs include:

> *Environmental Conservation,* Raymond F. Dasmann. John Wiley and Sons, New York, 1959.

> *An Ecological Approach to Conservation,* Russel L. Hamm and Larry Nason. Burgess Publishing Co., Minneapolis, 1966.

> *Teaching for Survival,* Mark Terry. Friends of the Earth/ Ballantine, New York, 1971.

> *Curriculum Enrichment Outdoors,* John Hug and Phyllis Wilson. Harper & Row, New York, 1965.

> *Integrating Conservation and Outdoor Education into the Curriculum (K-12),* William Stapp. Burgess Publishing Co., Minneapolis, 1965.

> *Manual of Outdoor Conservation Education*, Joseph J.
> Shomon. National Audubon Society, New York, n.d.

Most curriculum guides still tend toward old-style conservation. Representative efforts to develop man-in-environment guides include:

> *Guidebook for Education in Environmental Awareness*, The
> American Institute of Architects, Washington, D.C.,
> 1970.

> *People and Their Environment: Teachers' Curriculum Guide
> to Conservation Education*, Matthew J. Brennan. J. G.
> Ferguson Publishing Co., Chicago, 1969. The Ferguson
> Company also produces grade-oriented manuals relating
> to specific subjects (e.g., Social Studies, grades 10-12),
> under the same title.

> *Education for Survival: Social Studies and Science Cur-
> riculum Guide for Grades I, II, III*, published by North
> Jersey Conservation Foundation. Morristown, N.J., 1970.

Professional journals useful to teachers and administrators include:

> *Environmental Education.* See particularly "Environmental
> Encounters," William Stapp, Fall 1970; "Roles for
> Social Scientists in Environmental Education," Robert
> N. Saveland, Winter 1970; "Fundamental Concepts for
> Environmental Management Education (K-16)," Robert
> E. Roth, Spring 1970.

> *Grade Teacher.* See the January 1969 issue for a series of
> articles on "Ecology, Why You Must Teach It."

> *The Science Teacher.* See the September 1970 issue for a
> special section, "Developing an Environmental Ethic,"
> containing articles on public health, industrial pollution,
> architecture, and the status of environmental education
> in the public schools.

Teachers will find these special U.S. Government publications useful.

From Sea to Shining Sea, A Report on the American Environment by the President's Council on Recreation and Natural Beauty. Government Printing Office, Washington, D.C., 1968. This 304-page book surveys urban and rural environmental problems, and the complications produced by transportation systems. The last 100 pages are a guide to environmental reform action, with excellent resource listings (books, free films, and agencies).

Teaching Conservation Through Outdoor Education Areas, Forest Service, U.S. Department of Agriculture. Government Printing Office, Washington, D.C., 1968.

Education and Outdoor Recreation, Bureau of Outdoor Recreation. Government Printing Office, Washington, D.C., 1969.

Finally, special mention should be made of two book series containing excellent environmental education resources.

Life Nature Library, Time and Life Bldg., Chicago.

Our Living World of Nature Series, McGraw-Hill Book Co., New York.

Urban Problems

The degraded environments of our cities waste human resources, destroy social cohesion, and block environmental reform. Listed below is a core library for the park and recreation professional who would understand urban problems to seek their remedy.

The Conscience of the City, Raymond Aaron, *et al. Daedalus,* Fall 1968.

The City is the Frontier, Charles Abrams. Harper Colophon Books, New York, 1967.

Black Families in White America, Andrew Billingsly. Prentice-Hall, Englewood Cliffs, N.J., 1968.

Dark Ghetto, Dilemmas of Social Power, Kenneth B. Clark. Harper & Row, New York, 1965.

A Relevant War Against Poverty: A Study of Community Action Programs and Observable Social Change, Kenneth B. Clark and Jeannette Hopkins. Harper & Row, New York, 1968.

Black Ecology, Nathan Hare. From *The Black Scholar*, April 1970.

The Emergence of Metropolitan America, 1915-1966, Blake McKelvey. Rutgers University Press, 1968.

Urban Sociology, R. N. Morris. Praeger, New York, 1968.

Community Involvement, Clarence M. Pendleton, Jr. From *Parks and Recreation*, October 1970.

Racially Separate or Together?, Thomas F. Pettigrew. From *Journal of Social Issues*, XXV, No. 1, 1969.

White Power, Black Freedom: Planning the Future of Urban America, Arnold Schuchter. Beacon Press, Boston, 1968.

Special Publications and Periodicals

To answer the "But what can I do?" question, check these representative action guides:

Your Right to Clean Air: A Manual for Citizen Action, The Conservation Foundation. Washington, D.C., 1970.

The Environmental Handbook, edited by Garrett de Bell. Ballantine Books, New York, 1970. Ballantine is producing many action-oriented paperbacks for environmental reformers; check for new listings at your bookstore.

Ecotactics: The Sierra Club Handbook for Environmental Activists, edited by John G. Mitchell and Constance L. Stallings. Pocket Books, New York, 1970.

Guidelines for Citizen Action on Environmental Problems, Environmental Action for Survival (ENACT). Ann Arbor, Mich., 1970.

Two excellent and inexpensive information-action series are useful to environmental managers and communicators: The Problems of American Society paperbacks published by Washington Square Press, New York (with such titles as *The City as a Community, Air and Water Pollution, Poverty and the Poor, The Traffic Jam,* and *The People of the City*); and the Public Affairs Pamphlet series published by the Public Affairs Committee, Inc., New York (with such titles as *An Environment Fit for People, New Ways to Better Communities,* and *Humanizing the City*).

Most major periodicals have responded to environmental crisis with special sections (e.g., *Time, Saturday Review*) or expansion of traditional scope (e.g., *Natural History, Audubon Magazine*). For in-depth coverage of environmental affairs, see *Environment* and *Conservation Foundation Letter.* The Scientists' Institute for Public Information (SIPI) publishes *Environment* through the Committee for Environmental Information, 438 Skinker Blvd., St. Louis, Mo. 63130. This is an attempt by scientists to translate their environmental knowledge into laymen's terms. SIPI has also published nine workbooks for citizen action groups: *Air Pollution, Pesticides, Water Pollution, Hunger, Environmental Education, Nuclear Explosives in Peacetime, Environ-*

mental Effects of Weapons Technology, Environmental Cost of Electric Power, and *Law and the Environment.*

Conservation Foundation Letter (1717 Massachusetts Ave., N.W., Washington, D.C. 20036, issued monthly) concentrates each issue on a current environmental problem (e.g., SST, Corps of Engineers, government reorganization and budget allotments for environmental protection). This is a fine antidote to non-interpreted, superficial reporting of environmental issues.

Organizations

The growth in recent years of organizations involved or concerned with all or limited aspects of environmental affairs has outraced attempts to record them in any logical fashion or to analyze, effectively, their programs and services. Many old-line organizations, too, have revamped, redirected or expanded their programs to reflect increased awareness for *environment* in its broadest context.

An outstanding compilation of private organizations (and congressional committees and public agencies) at the national, regional, and state levels is the *Conservation Directory,* published annually and sold by the National Wildlife Federation, 1412 16th Street, N.W., Washington, D.C. 20036. This publication also lists key people in each group and notes the types of programs, services, and resource publications available.

Films

Most libraries have catalogues supplied by major film distributors — commercial, educational, and business-industry. Central film-reference services include the following.

American Institute of Architects
1735 New York Ave., N.W.
Washington, D.C. 20006

Carousel Films, Inc.
(Ecology Films Brochure)
1501 Broadway
New York, N. Y. 10036

U.S. Department of Agriculture
Motion Picture Service
Washington, D.C. 20250

U.S. Department of the Interior
(write to individual bureaus)
Washington, D.C. 20240

Encyclopaedia Britannica
Educational Corporation
425 North Michigan Ave.
Chicago, Ill. 60611

McGraw-Hill Films
(Environmental Films Brochure)
330 West 42nd St.
New York, N.Y. 10036

Michigan State University
Instructional Media Center
East Lansing, Mich. 48823

National Audiovisual Center
The National Archives
Washington, D.C. 20409

National Educational Television
Attn: Director of Information Services
10 Columbus Circle
New York, N.Y. 10019

The New York Times
(Environmental and Ecology Filmstrips)
229 West 43rd St.
New York, N.Y. 10036

Time-Life Films
4 West 16th St.
New York, N.Y. 10011

University of Michigan
Television Center
310 Maynard St.
Ann Arbor, Mich. 48108

University of California
Extension Media Center
Berkeley, Calif. 94720

Environmental Protection Agency
Office of Public Affairs
1626 K St., N.W.
Washington, D.C. 20462

U.S. Public Health Service
Audio Visual Facility
Atlanta, Ga. 30333

NOTES

NOTES

NOTES

NOTES

NOTES

NOTES

NOTES

NOTES

NOTES

NOTES

NOTES

NOTES